D0895741

P6-ABX-997

DO YOU HAVE A FRIEND WHO IS SUICIDAL?

Elizabeth Wahl

GOT ISSUES?

PAIN

SUPPORT

DEPRESSION

HELP

TENTION

Enslow Publishing
101 W. 23rd Street
Suite 240
New York, NY 10011
USA

enslow.com

Published in 2016 by Enslow Publishing, LLC.
101 W. 23rd Street, Suite 240, New York, NY 10011

Copyright © 2016 by Karen Zeinert
Additional materials copyright © 2016 by Enslow Publishing, LLC.

All rights reserved.

No part of this book may be reproduced by any means without the written permission of the publisher.

Library of Congress Cataloging-in-Publication Data

Names: Wahl, Elizabeth, 1961- author.
Title: Do you have a friend who is suicidal? / Elizabeth Wahl.
Description: New York, NY : Enslow Publishing, [2016] | Series: Got issues? |
    Includes bibliographical references and index.
Identifiers: LCCN 2015038014 | ISBN 9780766071919
Subjects: LCSH: Suicide--Juvenile literature. | Suicide--Prevention--Juvenile
    literature. | Suicidal behavior--Juvenile literature.
Classification: LCC HV6545 .W325 2016 | DDC 362.28--dc23
LC record available at http://lccn.loc.gov/2015038014

Printed in the United States of America

To Our Readers: We have done our best to make sure all website adresses in this book were active and appropriate when we went to press. However, the author and the publisher have no control over and assum no liability for the material available on those websites or on any websites they may link to. Any comments or suggestions can be sent by e-mail to customerservice@enslow.com.

Portions of this book originally appeared in the book *Suicide: Tragic Choice*.

Disclaimer: For many of the images in this book, the people photographed are models. The depictions do not imply actual situations or events.

Photo Credits: Cover, p. 1 Piotr Marcinski/Shutterstock.com (sad woman); p. 4 Ben Goode/ Hemera/Thinkstock; p. 5 Steve Granitz/WireImage/Getty Images; p. 6 iStock.com/Robert Ingelhart; p. 8 lassedesignen/Shutterstock.com; p. 10 Hulton Archive/Getty Images; p. 12 Zvonimir Atletic/ Shutterstock.com; p. 16 Gircke/ullstein bild/Getty Images; p. 18 CREATISTA/Shutterstock.com; p. 21, 72 wavebreakmedia/Shutterstock.com; p. 23 Steve Peters/The Image Bank/Getty Images; p. 25 Nikki Kahn/The Washington Post/Getty Images; p. 27 Bill Lawson/Shutterstock.com; p. 29 David Hume Kennerly/Getty Images; p. 31 Iculig/Shutterstock.com; p. 32 Photodisc/Thinkstock; p. 35 Dan Kosmayer Shutterstock.com; p. 38 OlegEvseev/iStock/Thinkstock; p. 40 Library of Congress Prints and Photograph Division; p. 44 THERESE FRARE/AFP/Getty Images; p. 47 Chamille White/Shutterstock.com; p. 48 Nottpossible/iStock/Thinkstock; p. 50 BananaStock/Thinkstock; p. 52 Dave Greenberg/Shutterstock. com; p. 54 fujji/Shutterstock.com; p. 56 Omaha Police Department/Getty Images News/Getty Images; p. 58 Ruslan Guzov/Shutterstock.com; p. 59, 69, 86 © AP Images; p. 61 Keith Philpott/The LIFE Images Collection/Getty Images; p. 62 VAUGHN GURGANIAN/AFP/Getty Images; p. 66 LUKE FRAZZA/ AFP/Getty Images; p. 74 iStock.com/Rich Legg; p 76 Sander van der Werf/Shutterstock.com; p. 77 iStock com/Nicholas McComber; p. 79 iStock.com/SolStock; p. 81 Clarence Williams/Los Angeles Times/ Getty Images; p. 83 Sabphoto/Shutterstock.com; p. 88 Dan Zak/The Washington Post/Getty Images; p. 91 Kathryn Scott Osler/The Denver Post/Getty Images; p. 92 Alex Garcia/Tribune News Service/Getty Images; p. 95 iStock.com/Chris Schmidt.

Contents

1

Suicide in the News

On August 11, 2014, the entertainment world was rocked by the news that comedian and actor Robin Williams had died at the age of sixty-three. Fans everywhere were saddened even further when it was confirmed that Williams had committed suicide. Apparently failing health and bouts with serious depression had led the beloved and talented comedian to hang himself.[1]

On January 4, 2014, newspaper headlines across the five boroughs of New York City shared the sad news that fifteen-year-old Amanda Cummings had died. Nearly a week earlier she had been critically injured after stepping in front of a city bus. In her pocket was a suicide note that stated she didn't want to live without her boyfriend, who had recently broken up with her. The day after Christmas, Amanda had confessed to her mother that she also was being bullied at school by jealous classmates. The next day, unable to bear all the hurt she felt, she purposefully stepped into the path of the bus, sustaining the injuries that would eventually kill her.[2]

On August 26, 2015, a former employee of television news station WDBJ in Virginia shot and killed a reporter and her cameraman while the two were in the middle of a live broadcast. The shooter, Vester Flanagan, killed himself while being pursued by the police.[3]

Fans worldwide were surprised when zany funnyman Robin Williams took his own life in 2014. Although it may have seemed like he had it all—riches, fame, and comedic genius—Williams was suffering inside, just like many other people.

News stories about suicide bring to light the grim truth that suicide occurs far more frequently than we think. In fact, approximately four people commit suicide every hour in the United States alone. That doesn't even account for those who simply think about it.

Also in 2015, a group of thirty taxi drivers attempted mass suicide in Bejing, China. The men gathered on a street in a busy shopping district and swallowed pesticide. None of the men died, but there is a long history of public suicide to protest conditions in China.[4]

These suicides and suicide attempts made the news because something about the deaths—the celebrity connection, the shocking nature of the deaths, or the sheer number of participants, for example—caught the attention of the public and the media. They sickened and yet, at the same time, somehow fascinated people. These deaths also reminded Americans that suicide is a common event in the United States.

Frighteningly Common

A 2014 report by the Centers for Disease Control indicated that as many as forty thousand Americans commit suicide every year. That is roughly one suicide every thirteen minutes. In the United States, killing oneself is the tenth-leading cause of death—and the second-leading cause of death in those ages fifteen to thirty-four.[5] Experts believe that the true number may be even higher, though, because many accidents may actually be suicides in disguise.[6] These numbers may not seem great, but killing oneself is so common that most of us at some point in our lives will lose a friend, a neighbor, a classmate, or a relative to suicide. In fact, in the time that it takes to read this book, several teens will try to kill themselves and one will be successful. Not only is a life forever lost, but also the anguish and despair that survivors—friends and relatives—feel can forever affect their lives, greatly increasing the effect of a single bullet or a dozen pills. So each time a suicide is reported, most Americans rail against taking one's own life.

Facing the Consequences

The following pages explore a variety of topics that surround the complex and controversial issue of suicide. Is suicide a modern phenomenon? If not, how has it been dealt with in the past? Which people are most likely to take their own lives? For what reason will they do so? How can we recognize—and help—people who might be thinking about ending their lives? Is there such a thing as an acceptable suicide? And finally, how can we help the survivors of the deceased when a suicide takes place?

Suicide Through the Ages

Thousands of years ago, in Ancient Egypt, an unknown person wrote a poem detailing the depths of his or her despair. The poet, who felt alone and alienated from others, hoped for death as a way to ease his or her suffering. As translated by Egyptology expert Thomas Eric Peet (b. Aug. 12, 1882–d. Feb. 22, 1934), the poem read, in part:

> To whom shall I speak today?
> Brothers are mean,
> One goes to strangers for affection . . .
>
> To whom shall I speak today?
> I am burdened with grief
> For lack of a [friend] . . .

Death is before me today
[Like] a sick man's recovery,
Like going outdoors after confinement . . .

Death is before me today
Like a man's longing to see his home
When he has spent many years in captivity.[1]

Whether this ancient person committed suicide is not certain. What is certain is that taking one's life was not uncommon in ancient times. One Egyptian writer claimed that so many of his countrymen were killing themselves by jumping into the Nile River that the crocodiles were becoming fat from feasting on their corpses.[2]

Acceptance or Trauma

Many ancient civilizations, in addition to Egypt, were confronted with the question of suicide. How each reacted to the concept of self-harm, as well as how each handled the situation once it had occurred, depended upon the particular culture involved. In Greece, for example, committing suicide was acceptable when one's health failed or when one was facing scandal and shame. Anyone contemplating suicide had only to convince local authorities that his or her death was a reasonable act. If the applicant was persuasive, he or she was given a carefully measured dose of poison to drink, which was guaranteed to bring about a quick death.

Suicide was also acceptable in India. When their masters died, slaves were expected to kill themselves to show unswerving loyalty to their owners. Likewise, a widow was expected to throw herself onto the burning pyre that cremated her husband's corpse, in effect burning herself alive. This practice, called *suttee*, continued well into the 1800s but is now outlawed.

Other ancient civilizations accepted suicide only during difficult times. When famine struck, some Inuit peoples hoped that older citizens would voluntarily end their lives so that younger people

Although it may seem like suicide is a modern phenomenon, it has been practiced across cultures throughout history. In India, particularly in Hindu communities, it was customary for a woman to kill herself soon after her husband's death.

might have a better chance to survive. The Japanese expected military leaders who had behaved in a cowardly fashion to kill themselves. In addition, some ancient civilizations accepted suicide, even mass suicide, in order to avoid enslavement. For example, in 73 CE, approximately 960 Jews who were besieged at Masada killed themselves rather than be taken prisoner by the Romans.

On the other hand, some ancient civilizations were appalled by suicide under any circumstances. The Baganda, who still live in what is now Uganda, believed that the spirit of a suicide victim suffered so much from the victim's traumatic death that it could not rest. Instead, it wandered about, angry and unhappy, seeking someone to punish. As a result, the bodies of suicide victims were burned in hopes of killing the spirit or wounding it to such a degree that it could do no harm.

Also, not everyone in an ancient society that approved of suicide accepted that society's generally held belief. In Greece, for instance, two famous philosophers, Plato and Aristotle, eventually spoke out against the practice. Plato thought that suicide was a cowardly act. In his opinion, Greeks had to learn to deal with their problems, not run away from them, an idea that is often repeated today. Aristotle believed that killing oneself was socially irresponsible because it deprived society of a vitally needed worker.

The Sin and Shame of Suicide

As part of their faith, Christians of ancient Rome believed that taking one's own life was more than sad or appalling; it was a sin against God. This stance was driven home by the theologian, or religious thinker, St. Augustine (b. Nov. 13, 354 CE–d. Aug. 28, 430 CE). As had the Greek philosophers before him, Augustine argued that suicide was socially irresponsible. He took matters further by declaring that suicide was "self-murder." Murder in any form was against God's commandments, and therefore an unforgivable sin in the eyes of the early Christian church. He proclaimed that there would be no asking for God's mercy once self-murderers met their maker in the afterlife, either. Life was a gift from God. Taking a life, even one's own, was the same thing as rejecting God's love. Being cast into hell was the price one paid when committing suicide.

When St. Augustine's arguments failed to put an end to suicides, the Roman Catholic Church, and later many Protestant churches throughout Europe, tried another tactic to make potential self-murderers think twice before killing themselves. Anyone who committed suicide would be denied a Christian burial. This punishment not only emphasized the seriousness of the crime but also would humiliate grieving family members who survived the deceased.

The condemnation of suicide as shameful, a sin, and even a crime can be traced to St. Augustine. In his book *The City of God*, the Christian theologian made the widely accepted assertion that killing anyone—including oneself—breaks God's commandments.

The shell of their body that was left on Earth would not fare much better. As punishment, the corpse of a person who had committed suicide was desecrated. Desecration involved driving a stake through the heart of the deceased and cutting off the hands, by which the dead person had taken his or her own life. The corpse was then buried under a pile of rocks at a prominent intersection near town to remind passersby about what happened to self-murderers. Some historians believe that burying these corpses near an intersection was also symbolic: The deceased had a choice, and he or she had taken the wrong road in life. Sometimes the deceased were stripped naked and dragged through the streets before being dumped outside of town, where vultures and crows would eventually pick the bones clean. This practice was common in parts of England, as well as the American colonies.

Illegally Dead

Unable to stop, or even stem (decrease) the practice of suicide, the government stepped in to pass laws against it. Since there was no way to prosecute those who had managed to kill themselves, the laws generally punished the deceased's survivors. For example, in England, Parliament passed laws that made it possible for local officials to claim all worldly goods left by anyone who took his or her life. In other words, the survivors of a suicide would lose their inheritance. The goal of the law was not so much to punish the survivors as it was to make people think twice before attempting suicide in the hope that hurting their loved ones would keep them from taking their own lives.

New laws also made it possible to arrest and punish anyone who survived a suicide attempt. Ironically, because suicide was listed as a serious crime, it was not unusual for officials to hang those who had tried to kill themselves. Although these laws were not strictly enforced after the 1700s, they remained on the books well into the twentieth century.

Romanticizing Death

While the Church and the government argued that suicide was a sin and a crime, a very different attitude took hold among some young artists and writers in the eighteenth and nineteenth centuries. Although death had long been a popular subject in art, suicide had seldom been portrayed, in part because it was viewed with such horror and disgust. Now young painters, novelists, and poets began to look upon suicide as both a romantic act and a dramatic way to make a statement.

The work that these artists and writers created was quite different from what the public had come to expect. In literature, for example, fictional heroes were sensitive men whose talents and works were ignored or laughed at by a hostile and ignorant public. Rather than change their standards to what the public wanted, the heroes killed themselves. Fictional heroines were often pictured as beautiful, brokenhearted lovers who had been rejected by callous cads or kept from their true love by cruel foes. Sometimes authors wrote stories about ill-fated lovers who committed suicide so that they might be together forever. In all cases, the dead were mourned with great fervor, usually by the same public, lovers, and foes who had rejected or hurt them.

The works of the Romantic writers, as they were eventually called, had a tremendous effect. One of the best examples of a Romantic writer's impact is the work of German writer Johann Goethe. One of his most popular novels, *The Sorrows of Young Werther*, is a series of letters written by a young artist named Werther, who is loosely based on Goethe himself. Through these letters, Werther tells a dear friend about his love for Charlotte, a beautiful woman who marries a man named Albert. Werther eventually kills himself rather than live without his love. Many young men throughout Europe, apparently unhappy in love as well, were taken by this sad story. They began to imitate Werther's dress—a blue coat and yellow vest—and his exaggerated sensitivity to events around

The Sorrows of Young Werther

Johann Goethe's book about Werther and his unrequited love for Charlotte was very popular, though critics claimed it promoted suicide. Below are several excerpts from the book, a series of letters written by Werther:

> *August 21*
> *In vain I stretch out my arms towards her. . . . Tears flow from my oppressed heart; and, bereft of all comfort, I weep over my dark future.*

> *September 3*
> *I sometimes cannot understand how another can love her so, dare love her, when I love nothing in this world so completely, so devotedly, as I love her, when she is my only thought, and I have nothing but her in the whole world.*

> *November 26*
> *I often say to myself, "You alone are wretched; all others are happy; no one has ever been tormented like you."*

> *December 20*
> *My mind is made up, Charlotte: I am resolved to die! . . . When you read this, my dearest, the cool grave will cover the stiff remains of that restless and unhappy man who, in the last moments of his life, knows no greater bliss than to [write to] you! . . . All is silent around me, and my soul is calm. . . . I wish to be buried in the clothes I wear at present; you have touched them. . . . The clock strikes twelve. So be it! Charlotte! Charlotte, farewell, farewell!*[3]

Johann Wolfgang von Goethe was criticized for romanticizing suicide, perhaps unwittingly, in *The Sorrows of Young Werther*. The novel's hero, who takes his life to end his despair over unrequited love, struck a chord with many readers.

him. Some even committed suicide. When they killed themselves, they were said to be suffering from Wertheritis.

In France, the idea of suicide became so popular at one point that some young adults formed suicide clubs. However, even though members claimed that they wanted to kill themselves, few actually did.

Suicide From a Scientific Standpoint

Near the turn of the century, in 1897, doctors and sociologists began to take a scientific look at the nature of suicide. Eventually called suicidologists, they did not so much reject the popular ideas that suicide was a sin, a crime, or a romantic gesture as favor a clinical, or scientific, approach. Some suicidologists believed that suicide was the result of mental illness. Others argued that physical causes, such as lesions on the brain, brought about suicide. A third group believed that social causes—poverty, for example—encouraged people to end their lives. Unable to reach an agreement about what brought about such deaths, during the next hundred years suicidologists became embroiled in heated debates and gathered information to support their arguments.

But even after more than a century of scientific study, many questions still remain. Therefore, suicidologists have continued their examination of the subject on a case-by-case basis. They sift through a growing pile of statistics, interview survivors of those who have ended their own lives, and study the lives of the deceased in detail. Like detectives, they hope to find answers—lots of answers—that will help them, and the general public, better understand suicide.

The Faces of Suicide

Virtually everyone knows of someone who has attempted or successfully committed suicide. That someone could be a celebrity whose work or life story made them feel like a personal friend. Sadly, sometimes the people who kill themselves actually are friends or loved ones. Teenagers are frequently offered grief counseling when students at their school or members of their class harm themselves. Chances are pretty good that any living individual may have considered or attempted suicide at one time or another.

The point is, suicidal behavior is not a problem specific to any one group or any one particular type of person. Studies conducted by suicidologists attempt to determine some of the people most likely to attempt or commit self-murder.

Recording the Rate

In order to determine how, and why, people commit suicide and who does it, suicidologists use what is known as a standard suicide rate. Interviewers determine how many people in a particular group—white men or black women, for instance—commit suicide in a certain year. Then, to make comparisons between groups easier, results are expressed not in total numbers of deaths, because different groups had different populations, but in the number of suicides per one hundred thousand members.

Suicide rates are reported regularly by the United States National Center for Health Statistics, usually using information from the Centers for Disease Control and Prevention (CDC). Unless otherwise noted, the rates and numbers given in this chapter are from the latest reports by the CDC.[1] These reports are based on 2013 data.

According to the CDC, the suicide rate in the United States was 12.6. This means that approximately slightly more than twelve and a half out of every one hundred thousand Americans killed themselves in 2013. This number has not varied greatly for several years. (For comparison, the World Health Organization lists Guyana as having the highest suicide rate (using 2012 data) at 43.22, while Saudi Arabia's 0.42 is listed as the world's lowest.)[2]

To put suicide into perspective, experts often compare the number of self-inflicted deaths with other causes of death in America. In 2013, approximately forty thousand Americans took their own lives. In comparison, more than 611,000 died from heart disease, nearly 585,000 died from cancer, and some 150,000 died from chronic lower respiratory disease, the three leading causes of death in the United States for 2013.

Gender Differences

When suicidologists first looked at years of data, one of the things they noted was that males were five times more likely than females to commit suicide. Unfortunately, not much has changed in that regard.

Finding the Standard

When suicidologists first set out to determine who committed suicide, why they did so, and how they did it, they encountered serious problems. Survivors, meaning friends and relatives, were reluctant to admit that their loved ones had committed suicide, due largely to shame and guilt. Also, since insurance companies did not pay death benefits when a person committed suicide, survivors usually tried to hide the truth, insisting that the suicides were actually accidents. Further complicating matters was the fact that early suicidologists used different methods to express their findings.

Establishing a standardized rate of suicides greatly increased the ease of recording self-murders for comparison, helping to put the issue of suicide more sharply into focus. However, suicidologists still struggle to get accurate statistics for these rates. This difficulty is due, in part, to the fact that old attitudes about suicide continue; therefore, some suicides are not reported. This is why experts believe suicide rates may actually be higher than reported. Even so, standardization helps experts identify trends and groups most at risk to kill themselves.

As of 2013, men were four times more likely to commit suicide, according to the 2015 CDC report. Out of the forty-one thousand Americans who killed themselves in 2013, more than thirty-two thousand were boys and men. The suicide rate for males was 20.6, while the rate for females was 5.7.[3] The vast difference between these rates does not mean that females don't try to kill themselves, however. In fact, girls and women are three times more likely than males to try to commit suicide. They just aren't as effective in their efforts. Also, females are more likely than their male counterparts to experience suicide ideation, which means thoughts of killing themselves.

An Ageless Dilemma

A significant difference between the sexes in regard to suicide was not the only pattern to emerge. According to suicidologists, members of certain age groups are more likely than others to commit suicide.

Few records of attempted or completed suicides made by children younger than five years of age have been recorded. But even though records do not exist, suicidologists believe that some children only three years old have tried to take their own lives.

Records for the next age group, children ages five to fourteen, have been kept and they are added to each year. These records indicate that this group has a very low suicide rate: one death per one

While much of the focus is on teen suicide, in reality adults have a much higher suicide rate. The latest data show that people aged forty-five to sixty-four are nearly twice as likely than adolescents to commit suicide.

hundred thousand children, according to 2013 numbers. Although these rates would not seem to demand attention, they represent a significant increase in self-inflicted deaths in this group since 1950. In fact, suicide was the third-leading cause of death among ten- to fourteen-year-olds in the 2015 CDC report.

Also according to the CDC's statistics, the next age bracket, ages fifteen to twenty-four, loses about five thousand members each year to suicide. The rate for this group is 11.1. Suicide is the second-leading cause of death for people in this age group, behind accidents and just ahead of murder. The suicide rate is even higher for adults, ages twenty-five to thirty-four (14.8) and thirty-five to forty-four (16.2). The rate for men is 24.8; for women, 5.9. This represents more than twelve thousand deaths. Accidents of all kinds—again, some of which are single-car crashes and may in fact not be accidents—and death from AIDS, a disease that destroys a person's immune system, are the major causes of death for this group, taking more than thirty-two thousand lives each year.

Americans ages forty-five to sixty-four also have a higher than average suicide rate, nearly eighteen per one hundred thousand people. The rate for men is 27.3, and the rate for women is 8.1. The last group, people over age sixty-five, are slightly less likely to take their own lives than they were decades ago. Since 1980, the number of elderly Americans who have chosen to die has grown. In 1980, the suicide rate for this group was 17.6. In 1988 it reached 20.9.[4] The most recent statistics indicate that the overall rate is 16.1. Older Americans made up about 14 percent of the total population in 2013, yet they accounted for 17.5 percent of the nation's suicides that same year.

It is interesting to note that when older Americans want to kill themselves, they are very effective at doing so. The ratio of attempted suicides to actual suicides among all Americans is 10:1, that is, out of every ten Americans who try to kill themselves, one will actually succeed. For young adults, the ratio is 100:1. For adults over the age of fifty-five, the ratio, according to one study, is 1:1.[5]

Elderly people (those aged eighty-five and older) have the second highest suicide rate in the United States. Experts attribute this phenomenon to failing health, death of loved ones, and loss of independence.

The Racial/Ethnic Divide

Until twenty-five years ago, Americans were classified as white and nonwhite for almost all studies. So until the mid-1970s, it was very difficult to determine whether one particular racial or ethnic group was more likely to commit suicide than another. Once Americans were separated by race, however, significant differences became apparent.

The rate for all whites was—and still is—approximately 14.9, above the national average. Even so, this group, which is made up of millions of Americans, accounts for most of the suicides committed in the United States. Of the forty-one thousand Americans who took their own lives in 2013, more than thirty-seven thousand were white. The vast majority of these suicides (28,943) were committed by men.

Black Americans, on the other hand, experience a low suicide rate. Whereas thirty-seven thousand whites took their lives in 2013, only slightly more than twenty-three hundred blacks did so. The majority of these self-murders occurred among black males (1,891), while black females accounted for 462 deaths. How much longer rates will remain low for blacks is not certain. Recent studies indicate that some groups are at great risk. For example, the rate for suicides among black teens has doubled since 1980. As early as 1970, a few researchers noted that Native Americans had a high suicide rate, 21.6 per one hundred thousand. By the late 1980s, the rate had climbed to 29. [6] The greatest number of suicides occurred among male teens and young adults. Today, the rate is 11.7. Studies indicate that the suicide rate among Hispanic Americans is 5.3. Hispanic high school students thought about, planned, and attempted suicide in greater number than black or white teens in the same age group. The rate of suicide for Asian and Pacific Islander populations rests at 6.

State and Region Suicide Rates

Suicidologists also study location, wondering whether the suicide rate varies from state to state, region to region, or between large

Suicide rates are highest among whites. But not far behind are Native Americans and Alaska Natives, whose suicide rates, particularly among male teens, are climbing steadily.

cities and rural areas. Their current findings indicate that Montana has the highest suicide rate at 23.9, more than twice that of the national average. Alaska is not far behind at 23.3. Rounding out the top ten for 2013, in descending order, are Wyoming, New Mexico, Utah, Nevada, Colorado, Idaho, Maine, and Vermont.

When suicidologists divide the nation into sections, they also note significant differences. The average rate for the western states is 14.1. The states with the lowest suicide rates are found in the Northeast (10.4). The Midwest and the South come in at 13.2 and 13.4, respectively.

For years, it was believed that people in small cities and rural areas committed suicide less often than people who lived in big cities. This was true seventy-five years ago when the average suicide rate in large cities was 17 and the rate in rural areas was 11. By 1991, though, there was little difference in the rate between city dwellers and their country cousins.[7] Things have gotten worse for teens living in small towns and rural communities. From 2004 to 2013, small towns and rural areas increased by approximately 20 percent. The smaller or more remote the community, the higher the chance of teens taking their own lives. In fact, the 2013 CDC report indicated that the risk for death by suicide was practically twice as high for rural teens (17.6) than it was for their urban counterparts (10.3).

Group Belief Systems

Over the years interviewers studied various religious groups as well. Because suicide had long been viewed with horror and disgust by many religious leaders, members of Christian denominations as well as members of the Jewish faith, interviewers were not surprised to learn that these groups had lower than average suicide rates in the past. Although some suicidologists believe that this trend continues today, this is difficult to prove. Death certificates do not have to indicate the deceased's religion.

Whereas some religious groups have been known for their opposition to suicide, others, which have been commonly considered

Teens in rural areas have a suicide rate nearly double the rate of their urban counterparts. Reasons cited are isolation, lack of access to health care, and a higher likelihood of firearm ownership.

cults, have committed mass suicide. Perhaps the most famous mass suicide took place in 1978, when more than nine hundred members of a religious cult died in Jonestown, Guyana, in South America. This group, consisting mostly of Americans, was led by Jim Jones, who had moved his followers from California to Guyana in 1977. Jones had several encounters with the law in Guyana, just as he had in the United States. When authorities began a formal investigation of some strange—and probably illegal—activities in the religious community, Jones panicked and ordered his followers, who had routinely practiced suicide drills, to kill themselves. After being told that they would be together in paradise, Jones's followers were given a drink laced with poison. Although the total number of deaths was over nine hundred, not all agreed to kill themselves. Some of the dead were murdered. Jones hoped to eliminate all members so that no followers would be left behind to talk about him. However, a few managed to escape.

A bit more recently, thirty-nine members of the group Heaven's Gate killed themselves on March 19, 1997. Heaven's Gate followers believed that the appearance of the Hale-Bopp comet was a sign indicating that all was ready for them. They thought that a spaceship that would take them to paradise was hidden in the wake of the comet. All they had to do to board this unseen ship was to shed their "containers," their bodies, so that their spirits could rise toward the comet.[8] A handful of former members followed suit days later.

Sexual Preference and Gender Issues

Suicidologists also have explored how the issue of sexual orientation affects the suicide rate. Lesbian and gay individuals, who are attracted romantically and sexually to members of the same sex, have long been thought to have higher suicide rates than their straight peers. The same is thought to be true of bisexuals, who are attracted to both sexes. Studies that confirm this are few and far between, however. Early on, interviewers discovered that it was nearly impossible to determine a rate for gays in America because many hid their sexual orientation out of fear of persecution.

One of the first extensive studies on this matter was ordered by the United States Department of Health and Human Services. In *A Report of the Secretary's Task Force on Youth Suicide*, interviewers concluded that an estimated 30 percent of completed youth suicides were committed by homosexuals.[9] This 1989 report was controversial. Opponents claimed that the suicide rate was greatly exaggerated in order to gain public support and sympathy for the gay community. However, statistics from studies done by the University of Minnesota Adolescent Health Program in Minneapolis and

In 1978, more than nine hundred people died as a result of self-poisoning. The mass suicide was directed by tyrannical cult leader Rev. Jim Jones, whose Jonestown community was under investigation.

the Los Angeles Suicide Prevention Center, both of which were completed before this report, also showed that homosexuals were at high risk.[10]

A more recent study, published in an electronic version of *Pediatrics* in 2011, seems to confirm the notion that increased rates of suicide are attached to the US gay population. The study showed that 21.5 percent of gay and bisexual teens had thought about or considered ending their own life. Only 4.2 percent of straight teens had the same thoughts and feelings.[11] The study also revealed that gender identification—how people feel inside, either male or a female, regardless of their sex at birth—matters as much as sexual orientation when it comes to suicide rates. A National Transgender Discrimination study, also conducted in 2011, reported that 41 percent of transgender teen respondents had attempted suicide at some point in their lives.[12]

Reasons for Self-Harm

Each person has unique thoughts and feelings, as well as his or her own life experiences. It makes sense, then, that each person who considers or commits suicide has his or her own reasons for doing so. Still, suicidologists have uncovered a number of situations that are highly likely to drive people to harm themselves. Depression and its possible causes—which include loss, stress, and isolation— are major factors in most suicides. Other factors include drug and alcohol abuse; social, religious, and sexual issues; and wishful thinking. Often a combination of factors can result in an attempted or successful suicide.

More Than the Blues

Life has its up and downs. For most people, the downs do not last long, perhaps lingering for a week or so. Such spells, sometimes called the blues, are normal and commonplace. But if the blues

Everyone gets sad or feels hopeless from time to time. We might refer to this state as "feeling blue." But for some people, the blues can last for an extended period and can affect their ability to cope with feelings and events.

become more intense or last for more than a few weeks, the cause may actually be depression, which requires medical attention and counseling.

According to suicidologists, depression plays a major role in most cases of suicide. There are several common signs and symptoms of depression:

- crying easily and often
- having little or no energy
- experiencing a dramatic change in sleeping habits
- belief that the future is hopeless
- belief by depressed people that they are worthless
- refusal to take care of themselves properly

Not all depression cases are typical. Sufferers sometimes mask, or hide, their depression. Instead of withdrawing or crying, they may act out, taking great risks, seeking punishment because they feel worthless. Young children may repeatedly throw tantrums, for example, and teens might resort to fighting or taking drugs. Another factor that has allowed some depression cases to go unrecognized is an old-fashioned belief about who gets depressed. Depression is more common than generally realized—one out of every four Americans will probably suffer from it sometime during his or her lifetime. Anyone, young or old, can be a victim of depression.

At a Loss

Psychologists and psychiatrists have discovered several factors that can bring about depression so severe that sufferers may just want to die. One cause of depression is significant loss—the death of a loved one, the end of a close friendship, or the loss of a job, for example. Suicidologists speculate that some people kill themselves because they no longer feel needed, nor do they command the respect that they once had. Men who feel this way and also are widowers are at an even greater risk of killing themselves.[1]

Whereas many people recover from depression on their own, some cannot adjust to their loss without help. Those who lacked confidence and self-esteem before their loss sometimes believe that life is hopeless without their loved one or that they are worthless because they have failed. This is especially true if someone pinned everything on a particular person or a certain goal. The thinking goes something like this: *If . . . was alive, if . . . would still be my friend, if I had won, . . . I would be a worthy person. Now without . . . , I am nothing.*

Victims of Abuse

Another possible cause of depression, and a cause of low self-esteem as well, is abuse, meaning repeated physical assaults and verbal attacks. These undermine a person's sense of worth. This is especially true if the abuse is meted out by the very people who are supposed to love the victim—parents, siblings, spouses, and in the case of elder abuse, children. Victims of abuse may assume that there must be a reason that they were attacked, that they either did something wrong or that there is something wrong with them. This can lead to feelings of guilt and shame and believing that they are unloveable.

The results of one kind of physical abuse, sexual assaults, were highlighted in a special study conducted by Dr. Angela Diaz, chief of adolescent medicine at Mount Sinai Medical Center in New York City. Her study found that girls who had been repeatedly sexually assaulted had experienced dramatic mood swings, chronic tiredness, and long-term insomnia—all typical signs of depression. More than 80 percent of the victims thought about committing suicide, and half of them tried to do so, often more than once.[2]

Verbal abuse can also cause depression. Despite the children's rhyme, "Sticks and stones may break my bones, but names will never hurt me," name-calling and insults can actually do quite a bit of damage. Those who experience repeated put-downs may end up feeling worthless for a long time to come.

Victims of abuse experience great anger at their tormentors. But because it is often dangerous for these victims, particularly

Whether it's physical or emotional, abuse can lead to depression and thoughts of suicide. Victims of abuse often feel helpless to break the cycle of depression, mood swings, anxiety, fear, anger, and low self-esteem.

The Bullying-Suicide Connection

Bullying is a form of abuse, more commonly referred to as harassment, that is a growing reason for many youth suicides in the United States. Examples of bullying include verbal threats and physical violence. It can be conducted in person or virtually online. Bullying results in depression, anxiety, and feelings of helplessness. These feelings can easily lead to suicidal behavior.

The CDC issued a report in 2014 stating that teens and children who have been bullied are at an increased risk of attempting or committing suicide. Perhaps more surprising is the fact that bullies themselves face a higher risk of suicidal thoughts and actions. The report also indicated that, typically, additional factors are present when a young person kills himself or herself. In other words, while being bullied may drive some young people to commit suicide, that alone is not usually the case.[3]

young children, to express their rage, they "swallow" it, aiming it at themselves. They belittle themselves and dwell upon their mistakes, often calling themselves clumsy or stupid. Anger directed inward is enough to cause serious depression.

Bad Brain Chemistry

Depression may also be caused by physical abnormalities. Dr. Neal D. Ryan and Dr. Joaquim Puig-Antich, who have worked with suicidal adolescents, noted that teens who tried to kill themselves had very low levels of the growth hormone produced by the pituitary gland. Other studies have indicated that some people who have become depressed and have committed suicide had a low level of 5-hydroxyindoleacetic acid, 5-HIAA for short, in their brain. This chemical is a by-product of serotonin, which is believed to regulate mood.[4]

Another study, conducted by Canada's Centre for Addiction and Mental Health in 2006, discovered that some people experiencing major depression have very high levels of the enzyme monamine oxidase-A (MAO-A) in their systems. MAO-A is believed to break down serotonin and another mood-altering chemical called norepinephrine, as well as the brain's feel-good chemical, dopamine. Researchers hope to study the causes for increased MAO-A levels in some people in order to form better measures to treat and possibly prevent major depression.[5]

Abusing Drugs and Alcohol

Another potential cause of suicide is drug and alcohol abuse. Although not all people who abuse drugs and alcohol commit suicide, the more they abuse these substances, the more likely it is that they will intentionally kill themselves.

Those who abuse drugs and alcohol do so to escape their pain or to feel better about themselves, and many may already be depressed. Drug abuse often becomes a source of conflict between the user and his or her loved ones. Also, abuse can cause users to withdraw into a make-believe world. As a result, they fail in school or lose their jobs. Conflict and failure can lead to depression or increase it if it already exists. In addition, although alcohol may make a person feel temporarily happy, in the long run alcohol is a depressant. When it is abused by people suffering from depression, it can further depress them, increasing feelings of helplessness and hopelessness.

Drug and alcohol abuse also reduces inhibitions, making it possible for users to take risks that they would avoid if they were sober—driving recklessly, for instance. According to the CDC, nearly thirty-four thousand people died in automobile accidents.[6] Experts wonder how many of these deaths were deliberate or possibly examples of risk-taking that turned deadly. Either way, the end result is the same.

Getting drunk or high can be freeing for those who need to escape their problems or depressive feelings. These effects are only temporary, however; long-term use will only create more problems.

Society and Suicide

One of the things that suicidologists study is history. Were there times when the suicide rate varied greatly from the average? If so, what was happening then? Suicidologists noted that the rate rose during times of great economic hardships—the Great Depression in the 1930s, for example, when more than one fourth of all workers could not find a job. However, when America was in peril and needed every hand possible—World War II, for instance—the suicide rate decreased. Also, suicidologists noticed that during times of social upheaval, when society in general was undergoing great change, Americans were more likely to commit suicide.

Among the many changes that Americans are experiencing today is increased mobility. More than one fourth of the population moves every five years. This results in the loss of friendships and close ties to extended family members, grandparents, and aunts and uncles. Sometimes moving from one place to another can be a "triggering event," the final straw, for someone who is already depressed. Suicidologists believe that deeply depressed children may take their own lives rather than face living in a strange new world.

Mobility also plays a role in the high suicide rate in certain states. Senior citizens are one of the most mobile groups in America, and it is not uncommon for older people in the colder climates in the United States to move to Florida or to the Southwest when they retire. Often, though, when a spouse dies, the survivor feels isolated, far away from relatives and lifelong friends. If the survivor is also experiencing serious health problems, he or she may decide to commit suicide.

The Effects of Stress

Another societal issue that plays a role in suicide is stress, especially in the home. Many families undergo great changes over the years in addition to moving about. Divorce and remarriage are common occurrences in today's society. Children may find themselves in the middle of a bitter divorce fight or living with stepsiblings, as well as a stepparent, none of whom they particularly like. The loss of the ideal of living happily with both natural parents is difficult for some children to accept, and they mourn their loss. Although divorce is not the only factor in the growing suicide rate among adolescents, it is a factor that has to be considered. An estimated 70 percent of children who commit suicide come from divorced families.[7]

Divorce and remarriage are only two things that cause stress in the American home. Sometimes there is little communication in families, and children feel isolated and unwanted. In other homes,

Suicide rates tend to spike when the economy is in distress. During the Great Depression, when many Americans were out of work and couldn't feed their families, the suicide rate rose to its highest recorded level.

children may be given a lot of attention and pressured to move to the head of their class, to be a star even if they aren't able to do so. Worse yet, parents in such homes may show signs of affection only when a goal is met. The results in both cases are misunderstanding, conflict, and possibly thoughts of suicide. In one decades-old study, Michael Peck and Robert Litman discovered that approximately 90 percent of young people who were suicidal believed that their parents did not understand them. A majority, 66 percent, of those who committed suicide had long been on bad terms with family members.[8] Not much seems to have changed on that front.

Cultural Connections

Cultural issues also play a role in suicide, putting some groups more at risk than others. Native Americans, for example, many of whom live on reservations, have one of the highest suicide rates in America. They also have serious alcohol and drug abuse problems and overwhelming poverty—factors that have been linked to an increased risk of suicidal thoughts and actions. The majority of suicides in this group are committed by teens and young adults who are trying to decide how to live out their lives. If they remain on the reservation, where few jobs exist, their futures will be difficult. If they leave the reservation, they leave their friends, family, and ancestral homeland—a painful decision at best.

Studies have indicated that the suicide rate for black American teenagers has increased steadily since the 1990s. At one time, experts at the Centers for Disease Control and Prevention believed that this increase might have been due to stress. Many young black men and women faced extreme pressure from their parents to achieve in school. Some in the black community regarded this as an attempt by some in their midst to be more like whites and, therefore, unacceptable. Consequently, black teens who excelled found themselves cut off from old friends. The result was a lot of conflict and stress.[9]

Trouble Spots for LGBT Individuals

Issues surrounding sexual orientation and gender identity can also play a role in suicide. Homosexuality has not been widely accepted in the United States over the years. Various studies during the 1980s and early 1990s revealed that more than half of the lesbians, gays, bisexuals, and transgenders (LGBT) who had been interviewed reported that they had been physically and verbally abused. Almost all in this group had been insulted prior to being beaten, robbed, or raped. To make matters worse, former friends refused to be seen with them. And a number of homosexuals had been cut off by their families when they told their parents and siblings about their sexual orientation.[10]

These same studies indicated that gay teens are more likely to commit suicide than older LGBT individuals. During the teen years, young people first become aware of their sexual preferences. It is also the time in life when young adults are trying to become more independent. As they gradually sever ties with their parents, teens seek a new support system—their peers. In order to do this, teens try to fit in, to be like everyone else. LGBT teens, however, are different from the majority. As a result, they are not always well accepted. On the other hand, if LGBT teens pretend to be something that they are not, the burden that they carry can be overwhelming. To avoid being discovered, they may shy away from making friends. It's no wonder, then, that so many LGBT teens report feeling isolated and lonely. This often results in depression and self-hatred—which can, in turn, lead to suicidal behavior.[11]

Sometimes LGBT individuals mask their depression with risky behavior. Several studies indicate that many LGBT teenage males get into trouble. They cut classes, run away, use drugs and alcohol, and some turn to prostitution to survive.[12] They also may engage in risky sexual behavior. Having unprotected sex can lead to contracting a sexually transmitted disease such as herpes. LGBT teens having unprotected sex also increases the chance that participants could be exposed to the HIV virus, which causes AIDS.

Since harassment, abuse, isolation, and risky behavior are issues faced by LGBT individuals, it is not surprising that the suicide rate for gays is high. According to some suicidologists, homosexually oriented individuals are two to three times more likely than heterosexuals in the same age brackets to kill themselves. Of note is the fact that not all experts accept the concept that the suicide rate for LGBT individuals is high or that there is a connection between homosexuality and suicide. Opponents of the studies attack the statistics presented by interviewers, arguing that until many more gays are questioned the conclusions are meaningless. These experts also point out that many factors play a role in teenage suicide, not just a person's sexual orientation or gender identity.

False Perceptions of Reality

Suicide can be the result of wishful thinking as well. Wishful thinking involves making decisions based on the way things people wish they were, instead of what is really happening in their lives. People who engage in this thinking kill themselves for very different reasons. Some may be trying to punish those who they feel have treated them badly. It is the "You'll really be sorry!" belief. Often these people arrange their deaths so that those who are to be punished will be the ones to find the body. Perhaps they use the gun of the person they want to punish or arrange their deaths so that those targeted to be punished actually witness the suicide.

Revenge is not the only motive for wishful-thinking suicides. Sometimes those who commit suicide have witnessed an outpouring of grief and compliments at a funeral. Experiencing serious problems and feeling worthless, some people may try to kill themselves so that they, too, may have a similar show of love and concern.

Celebrities make headlines when they die, especially if they kill themselves. Those who think of such celebrities as heroes may also decide to kill themselves. They do so to imitate the stars, to join them in the hereafter, and to gain publicity through their deaths that they couldn't achieve by living. They may believe that they will make history, but in reality, their behavior is simply another example of wishful thinking, for the publicity, just as the revenge or the outpouring of compliments, is short-lived at best. More important, the deceased will not be present to savor the moment.

Wishful thinking may also play a part in accidental suicides, deaths that were meant to be near misses. These suicides are usually caused by one of two things: Either the deceased wanted to draw attention to his anguish through an attempted suicide or he wanted to manipulate someone, to force him or her to do something. For instance, the deceased may have been trying to force someone to

Many teens idealize celebrities who have killed themselves, such as Nirvana frontman Kurt Cobain. Such hero worship may motivate a distressed young adult to take similar actions, hoping to achieve the same adoration bestowed upon the celebrity when he or she died.

marry him by threatening suicide. Unfortunately, such schemes can backfire, and what was to be a near miss ends up becoming a completed suicide. How many of the thirty thousand annual suicides that weren't supposed to end in death is not clear. What is clear is the fact that the causes of suicide are complex. To believe otherwise is yet another form of wishful thinking.

A Cautionary Tale

On March 11, 1987, four teenagers in Bergenfield, New Jersey—Cheryl Burress, seventeen; Lisa Burress, her sixteen-year-old sister; Thomas Olton, eighteen; and Thomas Rizzo, nineteen—decided to kill themselves. They drove to a vacant garage, closed the door, rolled down the windows in their car, and left the car's engine running. While they waited for the garage to fill up with carbon monoxide, a deadly gas, they wrote suicide notes.

Like other unusual suicide cases, this made the evening news all across the country. Although the teens were not the first to commit multiple suicide, they made popular the phrase "cluster suicides." But as reporters and investigators began to piece together the events that led to the four deaths, these suicides were not unusual aside from their number. Like many other suicides, all four of the deceased had become overwhelmed by personal problems. Both boys had serious drug problems, and the girls were struggling—unsuccessfully—with their mother's remarriage. In addition, all four showed signs of masked depression, and they had been acting out in school. Three had finally dropped out, and Lisa had recently been suspended.

Also, all four mourned the death of a close friend, Joe Major, who had died under mysterious circumstances a few months before. Major's death had been ruled an accident, but most of his friends thought that his fall from a cliff, several hundred feet high, was a suicide. Three of the four who died had been with Major when he went over the edge.

Copycat Suicides

Two days after the four teens in New Jersey died, two teens in Alsip, Illinois—Nancy Grannan, nineteen, and Karen Logan, seventeen—also killed themselves. They, too, had died in a carbon monoxide–filled garage. Also like the New Jersey teens, they had become overwhelmed by personal problems. Grannan and Logan had dropped out of school, and neither could find a job. In addition, both had been drinking heavily for several days before they killed themselves. They had probably been considering suicide for some time, but it wasn't until the news about the cluster suicides in New Jersey reached them—what experts call a triggering event—that they decided to take their lives in exactly the same manner. Their deaths were copycat suicides.

A 2014 study conducted by researchers at the New York State Psychiatric Institute concluded that there is strong connection between media coverage of teen suicides, particularly cluster events, and copycat suicides. The greater, and more sensational, the coverage of a teen or teens killing themselves, the more likely it is that other teens will be motivated to attempt suicide themselves. Researchers explained that the media coverage was not responsible for copycatting. Rather, stories in the press may simply push teens subject to other suicide risk factors closer to acting on their suicidal thoughts.

Unthinkable Acts

Methods of suicide tend to be as individual as the victims themselves. After careful study, suicidologists have managed to determine patterns and common factors involved in the majority of self-killings. Means by which a person commits suicide, the location and timing of the event, and whether or not he or she leaves a note are all factors that experts have studied.

Instruments and Means of Death

Suicidologists have identified at least forty different means that people use to kill themselves. The method that they select usually depends upon what is available but also varies according to gender. According to the National Center for Health Statistics (NCHS), the majority of those who commit suicide do so by shooting themselves. In fact, the latest statistics available from the NCHS show that a few more than half of all suicides were committed with some kind

By far, the most common method of carrying out suicide is by using a firearm: More than half of all suicides were committed by shooting. Guns are more frequently used by males, however, and by those over the age of sixty-five.

of firearm in 2013. Males are the most likely to use this method: 87 percent of gun suicides in 2010 were male. People age sixty-five and older had the highest rate of suicide by gun. The number of suicides committed by this age group using a gun in 2010 was 10.6 per one hundred thousand.[1]

The second most common method of killing oneself is by suffocation. This includes hanging and strangulation, as well as asphyxiation due to inhaling carbon monoxide or other toxic fumes. Suffocation accounted for about one-quarter of all US suicides in 2012.

Ingestion—taking poison or an overdose of pills—is the third most common method, with a 2013 suicide rate of 2.1. Pills are used most often by females—allegedly to avoid disfigurement caused by other, more violent methods such as firearms—and by physicians who have ready access to lethal doses. Drugs are also favored by the elderly who are taking medications for legitimate health concerns, some of which could be potentially deadly in large amounts or when used in combination with alcohol.

Drug overdoses are not always fatal, however. Drugs take time to work, so if the would-be suicide is discovered in time or if the person changes his or her mind, his or her life can often be saved. The fact that many females resort to overdoses to try to end their lives, whereas males use a much faster and more deadly means such as guns, may help explain why females are more likely than males to survive suicide attempts. A study conducted by the Harvard Control Research Center indicated that suicide by firearm is effective 85 percent of the time, while only 3 percent of suicide attempts by ingesting pills proved fatal.[2]

Other methods of dying by one's own hand include leaping from a great height, slashing one's own wrists, diving into a river to drown, or purposefully crashing automobiles.

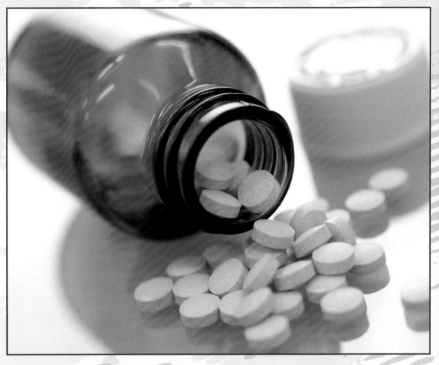

Ingestion of pills or a combination of pills and alcohol is the third most common method of suicide. Overdosing is considered easier and more peaceful, but it doesn't always result in death.

Choosing Where to Die

The place chosen by suicidal people often has a special meaning. A middle-aged single woman whose dream was to marry and have a family killed herself in her hope chest, which stored linens she had embroidered for her much-longed-for home once she got married. A grief-stricken widower killed himself beside his deceased wife's grave. A seriously ill opera fan killed himself by jumping from the top balcony in the Metropolitan Opera House. One young man, whose family had moved often during his short lifetime and was upset over the most recent move, hanged himself on a large oak tree behind his home. The suicide note he left behind indicated that he chose the tree because it had deep roots, something he believed that his family lacked.

Sometimes people choose a place known for suicide attempts, such as the Golden Gate Bridge in California. Since 1937, when the first person jumped to his death from the bridge, there have been more than seventeen hundred confirmed deaths from people jumping off the bridge. That number does not include attempted suicides or unconfirmed deaths, where a body was never found.[3] To some people, the bridge, with its beautiful surroundings, is a suicide shrine.

At the Appointed Day and Time

Popular myths about suicide include the false belief that suicidal people kill themselves in the middle of the night during the winter holidays, when everyone else appears to be happy and content. In reality, most suicides are committed in broad daylight in the month of May. Suicidologists believe that the sense of renewal and rebirth associated with spring and so evident in May is sometimes traumatic for suicidal people. They see new life all about them and yet feel that there is no opportunity for them to participate. The resulting pain is more than they can stand, so they kill themselves.[4]

During other months, suicidal people who plan their deaths long in advance may choose a date that has a special significance to them. One man killed himself on July 4, Independence Day, to symbolize his freedom from anguish and pain. A mentally disturbed woman who was deeply depressed over her daughter's upcoming wedding killed herself on the day of the wedding in the church where the vows were going to be exchanged. Others committed suicide on their birthdays.

Many suicides, especially among teens, are set to take place when family members are in the house. Spouses have been known to take a handful of pills shortly before their partners were expected to return home. Experts believe that these planned suicides are not suicides at all but rather dramatic calls for help.

San Francisco's majestic Golden Gate Bridge is the top site in America for those jumping to their deaths, despite offering a phone that connects directly to a crisis center.

The Last Outfit

Before the members of Heaven's Gate killed themselves, they put on special clothing, including black tennis shoes. Since all wore the same kind of clothing and were covered with unusual diamond-shaped purple shrouds, it is quite likely that these items had special meanings. Purple, for example, is used by various faiths as a symbol of spirituality.

Others who have killed themselves have sometimes donned their best clothing, assuming that they would be buried in it. A few chose a garment that reminded them of a certain event or person. In Goethe's romantic story about Werther, for example, the hero died wearing a jacket that his beloved had touched and admired.

People who are imitating the death of a star not only use the same kind of weapon that the celebrity used but also wear clothing that represents the star. When several girls killed themselves after singer Kurt Cobain took his life in 1994, they wore T-shirts with his name and likeness.

Slow Suicide

Because suicide still has a stigma attached to it, people who have what suicidologists call a "death wish" may try to kill themselves slowly, on what is sometimes referred to as the installment plan, or shadow suicide.

Like those who want to kill themselves outright, those who use the installment-plan method can do so in a variety of ways. Some might become heavy drinkers, consuming large quantities of alcohol until they destroy their livers. Others might smoke cigarettes until they develop lung cancer, a deadly disease, or they might take drugs. Others might eat too much, gaining far too much weight, putting strain on their hearts and clogging their arteries with fat. On the other hand, some might eat too little, depriving their bodies of much-needed nutrients. Some may drive recklessly and take chances that others would call crazy.[5]

Not all experts believe in slow suicides. They point out that it is not unusual for depressed and distressed people to seek solace—and not necessarily death—in alcohol, cigarettes, and food. Eating too little, they add, especially among young women, simply reflects our society's obsession with being thin. And driving too fast may be nothing more than carelessness. These experts also point out that sometimes depressed people remark that instead of experiencing intense emotional pain, they feel numb. Some of these patients deliberately seek out dangerous situations just to see whether they can once again feel something, even if it's incredible

Experts disagree about the notion of so-called slow suicides. Some believe that people engage in destructive behavior such as driving erratically or taking drugs with the intent that one day it will kill them. Others believe such behavior is an attempt to feel something.

fear. Suicidologists, however, agree that abusing alcohol and drugs or driving too fast are self-destructive acts that may lead to death, intentional or not.

A Note Before Leaving

Even though suicidal people always leave notes in the movies, in real life only one out of every five people who commits suicide leaves a message. One letter is the common number. Some people write several notes, perhaps sharing private thoughts with different individuals.

The content of suicide notes varies greatly. Because the people writing them are under great stress, it is not always possible to know whether they really meant what they said. In general, though, most of the deceased try to explain why they want to die. They may insist that no one else is responsible for their act, or they may list all whom they blame, giving numerous examples of mistreatment over the years. The following note was left by a sixteen-year-old boy named Jay. It is a good example of a message that tries to explain why someone wants to die. It also is a good example of the thoughts of a deeply depressed person. Jay wrote:

> Dear World,
>
> I don't want to get my hair cut. I don't want to tend kids or see Tina at school on Monday. I don't want to do my biology assignment or English or history or anything. I don't want to be sad or lonely or depressed anymore. I don't want to talk, sleep, move, feel, live or breathe anymore. Tina, it's not your fault. Mom and Dad, it's not your fault. I'm not free. I feel ill. I'm sad. I'm lonely.[6]

Some choose their words to hurt as much as possible. One young man who hanged himself next to the family Christmas tree had pinned a note to his clothing before he took his life. The note simply said: "Merry Christmas."[7]

family

I'm so sorry for what I've put you through I never meant to hurt all of you so much and I don't blame any one of you for disowning me I just cant be a burden to you and my friends any longer you are all better off with out me. I'm so sorry for this.

I've just snapped I cant take this meaningless existence anymore I've been a constant disappointment and that trend would have only continued. just remember the good times we had together

I love you mommy
I love you dad
I love you Kira
I love you Valancia
I love you Cynthia
I love you Zach
I love you Cayle
I love you Mark. (p.s. I'm really sorry)

Suicide notes can shed light on why a person has chosen to end his or her life. They can bring comfort to survivors or make them feel guilty. Sometimes they provide practical directions, as well.

A few suicide notes list the deceased's belongings and explain how they should be distributed. In some cases, the deceased may mail his or her notes along with some prized belongings, such as books or records, only hours before he or she takes his or her life. On a rare occasion, he or she may even select gifts—for an upcoming birthday, for example—before he or she takes his or her life.

6

The Death With Dignity Debate

No one likes to think of themselves or their loved ones lingering with a painful terminal disease. Yet helping someone die is considered unethical (not in line with normal standards of care by doctors) and immoral (against what is considered right or good, particularly in a religious sense). Since the 1970s, there has been heated debate about a person's right to die with dignity. The controversy began with discussions about whether people should be kept alive by artificial means. It moved to a different level when the public was asked to consider the legality, and morality, of assisted suicide.

Lead-in to the Debate

In 1975, twenty-one-year-old Karen Ann Quinlan took a handful of tranquilizers followed by several alcoholic drinks. Shortly after, she fell into a coma and was rushed to a nearby hospital. Her breathing was irregular, so doctors placed her on a respirator. When she did not regain consciousness, she was placed on a feeding tube as well. As soon as tests were completed, the Quinlans were told that Karen had suffered so much brain damage that there was no hope for even a partial recovery. Instead, she could remain in a coma for years before dying.

After weeks of agonizing discussions with specialists, the Quinlans finally asked the doctors to take Karen off the respirator so that she might die. In 1975, this was a shocking request. Karen's physicians were afraid of being accused of malpractice, even murder, and they absolutely refused to honor the Quinlans' appeal.

Joseph and Julia Quinlan are pictured leaving the Morristown, New Jersey, courthouse after a judge ruled that they could not disconnect their daughter, Karen Ann, from life support. Quinlan's case sparked the right to die controversy in the United States.

When they couldn't get help from the medical profession, the Quinlans took their case to a New Jersey court. They wanted the judge to order the doctors to remove Karen from the respirator. Their lawyer argued that keeping Karen alive was unconstitutional because it was nothing less than cruel and unusual punishment. An attorney for the state, who was assigned to protect Karen's interests, argued that removing her from the respirator would be murder, pure and simple. Karen's doctors were also represented in court. Their lawyer argued that no one knew beyond a shadow of a doubt that Karen would never recover, so they could not take her off life support.

The Quinlans lost the first round in court, but upon appeal, they were given the right that they sought. In a landmark decision in 1976, the New Jersey State Supreme Court ordered the doctors to remove Karen Ann Quinlan from the respirator, and only the respirator, which they did shortly after. Instead of dying, though, Karen, barely breathing on her own at times, lived another nine years.

The Quinlan case was just the beginning in a long series of legal battles for the right to die that spanned fifteen years. In 1990, a new case had entered the spotlight. That year the United States Supreme Court ruled that the parents of Nancy Cruzan, who was in a coma and had irreversible brain damage, had the right to have their daughter's feeding tubes removed so that she could die.

The Cruzan ruling set a national precedent. By the time the case was decided, 70 percent of all Americans supported the right to die. This was a dramatic change in viewpoint, for just twenty-five years earlier, only 35 percent believed that a patient, or his or her representative, should have the right to refuse treatment. Once the majority of people accepted withholding treatment from patients who had no hope of recovery, the public turned its attention to an even more controversial issue: assisted suicide.

Nancy Cruzan was kept alive in a coma because a court ruled her family did not have the right to decide her fate. The debate over Cruzan's right to die went all the way to the US Supreme Court and inspired the now-widespread practice of creating living wills.

Enter Dr. Kevorkian

After the Cruzan decision, Americans began to question what it meant to die with dignity. What if withdrawing medical treatment to let the irreversibly damaged die did not result in immediate death? Furthermore, what if terminally ill patients who were in unbearable pain wanted to die but were unable to commit suicide by themselves? Should someone be allowed to help them end their life?

While the public debated assisted suicide, Dr. Jack Kevorkian took action. In 1990, the same year that the United States Supreme Court ruled in the Cruzan case, Kevorkian helped Janet Adkins,

Dr. Jack Kevorkian, pictured here after sentencing for a murder trial, became synonomous with the right to die. Called "Dr. Death" by the media, Kevorkian claimed to have participated in more than one hundred physician-assisted suicides.

a fifty-four-year-old woman from Oregon who suffered from Alzheimer's disease, commit suicide.

Adkins and her husband traveled to Michigan, where Kevorkian lived, to receive the doctor's aid. When they met, Kevorkian asked Adkins a few questions, decided that she was able to make decisions for herself, and discussed how she would die. In this case, Kevorkian favored death by asphyxiation, and he explained how it was to be done.

On June 4, 1990, Adkins climbed into the back of Kevorkian's van in a state park, lay down on a cot, and waited for the carbon monoxide flowing into the van from a hose connected to the exhaust pipe to kill her. Kevorkian turned her body over to authorities for an autopsy before announcing her death to a stunned public.

Expanding His Services

Kevorkian then set out to find others whose suicides he could assist. Newspaper ads were one means of finding more patients. One ad read: "Oppressed by a fatal disease, a severe handicap, a crippling deformity? . . . Show him proper compelling medical evidence that you should die, and Dr. Jack Kevorkian will help you kill yourself, free of charge."[1]

In addition to the carbon monoxide hookup, Kevorkian invented a suicide machine that patients could use. This device consisted of a stand with long plastic tubes and needles connected to three separate containers, each filled with a different liquid: a saline solution to enable the other fluids to enter the bloodstream more easily; a sedative to calm the suicidal person; and potassium chloride, a poison, to end the person's life. When the needles were inserted into a vein and a lever was pressed, death followed shortly after.

During the next eight years, Kevorkian claimed to have helped at least one hundred people kill themselves. Some Americans regarded him as an angel of mercy. Others, horrified by the mounting numbers, began to call him Dr. Death and worse. Legal authorities in Michigan, where all of the deaths took place, called him a murderer. They wondered aloud how some of his applicants who were paralyzed could have operated the suicide machine by themselves or climbed into the back of his van.

Prosecutors in Michigan also questioned the standards that Kevorkian used for accepting patients. Autopsy reports indicated that some of the deceased did not have serious health problems. For example, reports showed that Kevorkian's thirty-third patient, Rebecca Badger, who insisted that she had an advanced case of multiple sclerosis, was not seriously ill. Instead, when medical authorities questioned the doctor who diagnosed Badger's illness, he admitted that he had been deceived by her. After her death, he had learned that Badger had a long history of drug addiction. She also possessed the medical knowledge needed to convince doctors that she was sick and in need of the painkillers, to which she was addicted.[2]

Besides questioning Kevorkian's standards for acceptance, prosecutors questioned his methods as well. When rumors surfaced that one of his patients tried to change his mind at the last minute but was not allowed to do so, authorities took an even closer look at the doctor's activities. Eventually they decided that they had enough evidence to arrest and try him.

Taking "Dr. Death" to Court

Kevorkian was tried a total of five times in Michigan. At the first four trials, relatives of the deceased testified that their loved one was in agony and wanted to die but was unable to so without help. Kevorkian was acquitted in the first three cases, and the fourth ended in a mistrial. For the fifth trial, Kevorkian was charged in the death of fifty-two-year-old Thomas Youk. Suffering from amyotrophic lateral sclerosis (ALS, also known as Lou Gehrig's disease), an ultimately fatal disease of the spinal cord, Youk had requested Kevorkian's assistance in killing himself. In March of that year, Kevorkian was convicted of second-degree murder. He was

A Grisly Side Business

Kevorkian had long talked about performing experiments on the dying and harvesting organs—hearts, livers, lungs, and kidneys—from his patients. On June 7, 1998, Kevorkian began the second phase of his assisted-suicide program: he supervised the removal of kidneys from Joseph Tushkowski, a quadriplegic who had been paralyzed for twenty-one years. After dropping off Tushkowski's corpse at a local hospital, Kevorkian announced that he had two kidneys to donate. He also indicated that there would be more to come in the future. He said, "Just as Janet Adkins was the first, this is the first of the line."[3]

There were a number of medical and ethical issues involved with this scheme. No reputable hospital or transplant facility would accept Tushkowski's kidneys, and it was highly unlikely that any other organs harvested by Kevorkian in the course of assisted suicide would be either. In the end, many deemed the doctor's organ harvesting business a publicity stunt to bring attention to his "attended" suicides.[4]

also convicted of delivery of a controlled substance, which was used to make the lethal injection.

Kevorkian was sentenced to twenty-five years in prison. He wound up being released on good behavior after serving only eight years. His medical license had been revoked, and he promised not to assist in any more suicides.

Getting the Word Out

While Dr. Kevorkian's assisted suicides grabbed headlines, a group known as the Hemlock Society worked quietly behind the scenes to help the terminally ill kill themselves. The organization, started by Derek Humphry in 1980, was named after the poison given to Greek citizens to end their lives. The society has promoted its

Founded in 1980, the Hemlock Society supported the passage of legislation that legalized physician-assisted suicide in the United States. Now known as Compassion & Choices, the organization's mission is to improve patient rights, particularly at the end of life.

cause primarily through a newsletter called the *Hemlock Quarterly*. This publication talked about suicide in general, accepted letters from subscribers who argued for assisted suicide for terminally ill patients, and printed testimonials of those who had helped a loved one die.

In 1988 the society decided to stop talking about suicide and tell subscribers exactly how to do it. One of the *Quarterly* issues contained a list of drugs that could kill if taken in large enough doses. It then listed the deadly amount needed. Because almost all of the drugs listed were regulated medications and required a prescription from a doctor, the newsletter gave tips on how to obtain the medicines, including faking an illness and smuggling drugs from abroad.

The society also began to offer legal advice if subscribers were arrested for helping someone die. From the beginning, the society was not only successful in winning cases in court but was also able to gain more and more supporters. By the mid-1990s, the Hemlock Society had almost forty thousand members. As the demand for information about suicide continued to grow, Derek Humphry wrote *Final Exit*, his now famous book about how to commit suicide. It was so detailed that Humphry believed that anyone who followed the directions could commit suicide or aid in an attempt. This book became a best seller in 1991.

Northwest Passage of a Suicide Law

Demand for Dr. Kevorkian's help and the growing membership of the Hemlock Society, as well as the publication of Humphry's book, caused quite a stir everywhere and led to a debate about legalizing assisted suicide. The results were very different in different states. While Michigan legislators tried to write a law that would stop Kevorkian, citizens in California, Washington, and Oregon voted on laws that would permit physician-assisted suicide. Voters in California and Washington rejected the idea, but in Oregon in 1994 the electorate passed Initiative 119, which paved the way for the first law in America that made physician-assisted suicide legal. The Death with Dignity Act (DDA) squeaked by after receiving only 51 percent of the votes.

Once the initiative had passed, legislators set out to write a law that would do three things. First and foremost, it would help patients with less than six months to live end their lives when they wished to do so. Second, it would make these suicides as easy and as painless as possible. Third, it would make sure that the DDA had very specific limits to prevent abuses.

To achieve these goals, legislators included a number of safeguards to protect patients. Applicants must make a written request for help. They are then interviewed by two doctors, who look for signs of depression and examine each applicant's medical records. The doctors also explore the possibility that applicants are being pressured to die because of mounting medical bills or exhausted caregivers. If the doctors believe that the applicants are acting only out of depression or are unable to make an informed decision or do not really want to die, assistance is denied. If assistance is offered, applicants must then undergo a waiting period of fifteen days—time to really think about their decision.

At the end of the waiting period, a physician can write a prescription for a lethal dose of medication and give specific instructions on how to take it. This ensures as quick and as painless a death as possible. To make sure that an applicant has every opportunity to change his or her mind and that the act is suicide, not murder, the patient must take the pills; no one else may administer them.

Only residents of Oregon may request assistance. This eliminates the possibility of turning Oregon into a suicide mecca. Also, doctors who choose to participate in the program must be licensed in Oregon and follow the state's rules. Records have to be available for examination at any time.

Under Oregon's Death With Dignity Act, an adult resident diagnosed with a terminal illness that will lead to death within six months may be prescribed medication that will end his or her life.

Working Against Oregon's DDA

As soon as the law was passed, opponents appealed to the courts to strike it down, leaving the act on the books but unable to be used. Primarily led by church groups and right-to-life leaders, the opposition believed that assisted suicide was morally wrong. They referred to long-held beliefs by religious leaders: suicide, assisted or self-inflicted, was nothing less than murder; suicide was a rejection of God's gift of life and, therefore, God; and finally, suicide was the act of a mere mortal who was trying to make decisions that only God should make. Also among the opponents to the Death with Dignity Act were many doctors. They argued, as had the doctors in the Karen Ann Quinlan case, that physicians were expected to preserve life, not take it. Furthermore, they worried what assisted suicide might do to the trust between physician and patient, which was so necessary for good medical care.

Some opponents believed that assisted suicide could lead to early deaths for defenseless victims. Their concerns centered on hastening, or hurrying, a patient's death for reasons other than those having to do with compassion. For instance, family members who stood to inherit from a terminally ill patient might convince that person to speed up the dying process for their own gain. Perhaps other patients might choose assisted suicide mainly to save their loved ones the expense and emotional stress of waiting for their demise. In addition, more than a few opponents worried about the potential for doctors to make mistakes—as had been the suspected case with at least one of Kevorkian's patients.

Legal and Legislative Battles

While opponents in Oregon attacked the bill publicly, they continued to put the issue before judges, hoping one of them would strike down the act. As the case moved through the courts all the way to the United States Supreme Court, these opponents followed assisted-suicide cases in other states, especially *Glucksberg v. Washington State* and *Quill v. Vacco* (New York State), in which Dr. Harold Glucksberg and Dr. Timothy E. Quill were challenging their own states' bans on assisted suicide. They argued that Americans had a constitutional right to end unbearable suffering with a doctor's help. Both of these cases reached the Supreme Court in January 1997. On June 26, 1997, the Court issued its opinion: the justices denied a sweeping right to assisted suicide, which supporters of assisted suicide had sought, and allowed the laws banning assisted suicide to stand.[5]

At first this appeared to be good news for opponents of assisted suicide in Oregon. However, on October 15, 1997, the Supreme Court refused to hear arguments concerning the DDA, dashing opponents' hopes of any court support. Chief Justice William

Rehnquist announced, as he had in the Washington and New York cases, that the issue of assisted suicide should be decided in the public arena.[6] The citizens of Washington and New York had outlawed assisted suicide of any kind; the citizens of Oregon had voted to legalize a very limited procedure. The Court's refusal to hear the case made it possible for Oregon physicians to begin to provide assistance to terminally ill patients who wished to commit suicide.

Opponents refused to give up, though. They had already persuaded the state legislature to ask Oregonians to vote on the DDA again. Ballots were mailed on October 16, 1997, as previously planned, one day after the Supreme Court's decision. When citizens voted again for the act, this time by a larger margin, opponents sought other means to abolish the law. To date, all efforts have failed, including a special appeal to the United States attorney general.

Where the Situation Stands

In 2008, Washington State passed its own Death With Dignity Act, and Vermont passed the Patient Choice and Control at End of Life Act in 2013. Montana courts have ruled that there is no policy forbidding assisted suicide in that state; therefore the issue can be used as a defense in court, making the practice technically legal.[7] In 2014 a New Mexico court ruled that assisted suicide was legal, but the ruling was struck down by the state's Court of Appeals in 2015.[8]

Left Behind

It may rightly be said that there are multiple victims of suicide. There is, of course, the person who kills himself or herself. But then there are the survivors, the family, friends, and others connected with the suicide who are left behind. Feelings of confusion and guilt mingle with grief in a survivor's mind. Often survivors are in need of counseling as much as those who have thought about or attempted to commit suicide.

"I Should Have Done More"

Although any death is painful for survivors, sudden death may be especially hurtful, because there is no opportunity to say good-bye or to resolve conflicts. For suicide survivors, these unresolved issues often take on a special meaning. Survivors sometimes see existing conflicts as the reason for their friend's or family member's suicide—in effect, blaming themselves for their loved one's death.

This assumption is sometimes reinforced by people in the deceased's community. Because suicides are more newsworthy and create more curiosity than most deaths, they are often highlighted by the media. Therefore, it is not unusual for strangers to point to survivors or even to question the mourners. Sometimes the questions are cruel. One mother was actually asked—repeatedly—"What did you *do* to her?" after her daughter committed suicide.[1] The result was overwhelming guilt.

Also, survivors may repeatedly review past events, looking for any clue that might have predicted the suicide. If they recall even the slightest sign that their loved one thought about dying, they berate themselves for not having reacted to it quickly enough. If they don't find a clue, they put themselves down for not being intelligent or sensitive enough to have spotted the deceased's anguish.

Misplaced Rage

In addition to guilt, suicide survivors often feel anger, even rage, toward the deceased. This anger comes from a feeling of abandonment, of deliberately—and dramatically—being left behind. Anne-Marie, a young woman whose brother killed himself, said:

> I scream, I yell out the window. . . . I have never felt this angry in my whole entire life. Angrier than I ever was at my mother or my father for not being there. It's so frustrating! Because I always had . . . my brother. . . . I keep thinking, why did you do this to me?[2]

Left unresolved, this anger can lead to more problems. Some survivors lash out at others, accusing them of causing the deceased's death, making others feel guilty. Anne-Marie, for example, blamed her sister-in-law for her brother's death. "I have *hatred* toward my sister-in-law," she stated, "intense hatred."[3] Venting their rage at others often strains relationships to the breaking point at the very

Suicide ends a person's suffering, but the pain continues for that person's family and friends. Those left behind face confusion, guilt, and depression, often for the rest of their lives.

time that survivors need contact with other people. On the other hand, bottling up anger can lead to depression.

Shock and Awe

Because suicide is violent, it sometimes traumatizes, or shocks, those who are left behind. This makes it very difficult for them to deal with their loss. They can't concentrate or sleep, and they feel helpless. Although this is not unusual for anyone who has lost a loved one, suicide survivors may have an additional emotion: fear. They constantly worry that someone else they love will kill themselves as well. Their fears are not unfounded. Survivors are eight times more likely to attempt suicide than the typical American. Counselors believe that once one family member has committed suicide, other family members see it as an acceptable way to end their agony.

While survivors are learning how to cope with their trauma, they are under so much stress that they are physically at great risk. Survivors are prone to ulcers, high blood pressure, heart attacks, and accidents. Some turn to drugs or alcohol to ease their pain, creating even more problems. Counselors estimate that it often takes suicide survivors as long as three years to come to terms with their feelings.

Because their emotional scars are many and deep, some survivors find it impossible to heal. As a result, the traumatic event haunts them for the rest of their lives. This is especially troublesome for young survivors who have many years ahead of them. One survivor said, "When I was 16, my father shot himself. I am now 77 . . . and I am still not over it."[4] Another recalled:

> My father committed suicide when I was 11. Five years later, my brother did the same—with his police revolver. He killed not only himself but his wife and their two young sons. None of this made sense to anyone who knew him. Now, 30 years later, it still doesn't make any sense. . . . The pain . . . never goes away.[5]

Dealing with the trauma of losing a loved one by suicide can take years. It's no wonder that many of those left behind end up taking their own lives.

Trouble Finding Assistance

Since a stigma is still attached to suicide, survivors seldom receive the support from their community and even friends that they might have had under different circumstances. The lack of support may hamper a survivor's ability to heal. A woman whose son killed himself said, "Losing my son was painful enough, but the whispers . . . being avoided, having people not look me in the eye, or acting like nothing happened, never mentioning the death, changing the subject . . . is almost worse."[6]

Furthermore, because a suicide is so painful, family members sometimes refuse to deal with the death. One survivor said,

Along with the shock and sadness accompanying the suicide of a loved one, many people must cope with being a topic of neighborhood gossip or being avoided altogether.

"Nobody in the family wants to talk about it. You have to pretend that something terrible didn't happen."[7] Often in such situations, the deceased's room is kept exactly as it was, as if he or she might return anytime. In other cases, everything belonging to the deceased is packed and stored away, as if he or she had never existed. In either case, family members are forced to deal with the loss individually. This is difficult to do, especially for children, who have the fewest skills and life experiences to handle such a traumatic event.

Children Who Have Lost a Family Member

Children who lose a parent to suicide are at great risk for serious emotional problems. For many, the loss of a parent is their first experience with death, and they are completely unprepared to deal with so great a loss. In fact, very young children find it hard to even express their feelings at such a time. Teens, who are trying to establish their independence, do not necessarily want to talk about the event with adults, and few of their friends are likely to have had any experience with suicide. This makes it difficult for young survivors to get the support they need. Also, because teens want to be like everyone else and a suicide in the family sets them apart, teenage survivors may even try to deny their grief, which can result in depression.

Family members, hoping to spare young children, may not tell the children the whole story. The children respond by making up their own version of what happened. In most cases, they assume that it was something that they did—or didn't do—that led to their parent's death. If they had been better children, they reason, their father or mother would not have wanted to leave them. Sometimes they believe that they are so bad that they are unlovable. They react by withdrawing from friends and relatives at the very time that they need support. The situation is made much worse if the child is the one who finds the parent's body, since trauma is added to any guilt he or she feels.

Parents of suicide victims are often so enveloped in their grief that they cannot help their remaining children cope. Young sibling survivors may feel both neglected and overprotected.

The suicide of a brother or sister can be as painful for children as losing a parent. In addition to struggling with their grief and worrying that something they said or did caused the death, young survivors may also experience extreme jealousy when they see their parents grieving for the deceased. Mom and Dad, they reason, really did love my dead brother or sister best. Also, it is not uncommon for parents who have lost a child to become overprotective of their remaining children. Therefore, the surviving children may never learn how to become independent, self-sufficient adults.

Survivors of an Assisted Suicide

Great sympathy has been generated over the years by highly publicized court cases that were fought by family members for the right of a terminally ill person to die. Because these patients had no hope of recovery—unlike deeply depressed teenagers—many people can accept their decision to die. So survivors of these deaths usually do not experience the guilt or intense anger at the deceased that overwhelms most survivors of suicide. This doesn't mean that these survivors don't experience anger, though. In cases such as this, survivors' anger is usually directed at the living, not the deceased.

Sometimes survivors of assisted suicide are made to feel that they must defend the deceased's decision and, on occasion, even assisted suicide in general. Jonathan Smith's fight to defend his mother's decision to die is but one example. In 1989, Mrs. Smith was dying from fallopian cancer, an especially painful disease. Eventually she refused to eat, in order to hasten her death. This was done with her doctor's approval. Jonathan Smith, who was only eighteen years old at the time, was not only upset by questions he faced then but also continues to be upset whenever someone questions an assisted suicide. In 1997, he wrote an opinion piece for the *Milwaukee Journal Sentinel* titled "How Dare You Judge My Mom's Decision to Die." It read, in part:

> I get a little incensed with those who [pretend] to know better than those who are suffering as to what is right and moral. Such attitudes [belittle] the integrity, character and memory of my mother, and there is not one person on earth worthy of doing so. . . . To those who would . . . pass judgment upon others who suffer, I suggest that you get to know those who are suffering. . . . Don't you dare pass judgment without . . . understanding their experience.[8]

Help Is on the Way

Until the mid-1970s, very little help was available for suicide survivors. But when experts who specialized in suicide prevention began to realize that survivors were highly likely to kill themselves as well, they suddenly took an interest in those left behind. As a result, prevention centers began to offer counseling services to suicide survivors.

Next, a few survivors decided to follow a national trend in the 1970s and start self-help groups. They established organizations, such as Survivors of Suicide, held meetings, and invited other survivors to join them, to share their feelings with people who really understood their pain. Some of these meetings were presided over by survivors; others were led by mental health professionals.

In 1980, Survivors of Suicide held its first national conference. It was followed by many more. These meetings drew attention to the issue of suicide and enabled leaders of the conferences to educate

Thanks to efforts over the past decades in suicide prevention, help is easy to find. This includes assistance for suicide survivors. Hotlines, chat rooms, and support groups are all readily available.

Reaching Out to Survivors

It is a sad fact that just about everyone, at some time during his or her life, is likely to know someone who is a suicide survivor. It is important to know how to comfort these people. Below are some suggestions from grief counselors.

- Show concern. Attend the wake, visitation, funeral, or memorial service. A public show of support is important to grief-stricken survivors. If possible, offer your condolences at the service. A handshake, a hug, or a simple "I'm so sorry" means more than you can imagine at such a time. If you can't attend a service, send a card, call the family, or make a contribution to a memorial fund.
- Listen. Listen. Listen. Survivors need to vent their feelings. To do this, they need to talk about what happened, and they need people who will listen—and not judge—what they say.
- Offer to run errands. Sometimes survivors are too numb to do everyday errands. Volunteer to pick up groceries, take them to appointments, or to bring friends to the house to visit.
- Check on their physical well-being. Are they eating properly? Are they getting exercise? Do they need to see a doctor?
- When appropriate, help them find counseling.

the public about self-inflicted death. Leaders at the meetings also created a network of support services for survivors. As a result, today's survivors can receive help no matter where they live. They can call local suicide hotlines or contact clergymen, school counselors, or funeral directors.

Social workers at hospitals and in clinics can provide information and help as well. No one has to struggle with his or her feelings alone. There is life after death, and there are people willing to help survivors find it.

Prevention and Treatment

Survivors are certainly not the only ones who need help in dealing with suicide. Imagine the lives that might be saved if every person who ever attempted or even thought about suicide experienced an intervention and got the help he or she so desperately needed.

The Evolution of Suicide Help

Suicide prevention and treatment are relatively new concepts. Until the twentieth century, fear was the major weapon used to keep people from trying to commit suicide. Religious leaders warned followers that all who took their own lives faced an eternity in hell. Those who tried to kill themselves but failed in their attempt were threatened with legal prosecution, as well as scorn and contempt from their neighbors.

Beginning in the 1800s, prevention often included confining those attempting suicide to mental institutions. Even though, on average, only a percentage of suicidal people are legally insane (unable to make rational decisions), many doctors of the time believed that all suicidal people were mad. They were sent to live in institutions that were little more than warehouses for mentally ill people, many of whom were dangerous or simply screamed and shouted for hours on end. The scene at these places likely made some attempters more suicidal than ever.

Finally, in the early 1900s, a few brave souls began to think of suicide as a worthy area of study. They saw suicidal people as human beings, not hell-bound sinners who were crazy to boot. Social workers and counselors began to develop programs to prevent suicide attempts and to help attempters who survived. Most important of all, counselors did not resort to using scare tactics—which had failed for hundreds of years—to try to keep people from killing themselves.

Leading the Way

One of the first professionals to work in the prevention field was Harry Marsh Warren, a Baptist minister. In 1906 he started the Save-A-Life League in New York City. As a minister, Warren had been asked to counsel people who had tried to kill themselves. He quickly realized that many attempters had mixed feelings; they wanted to live, but they saw no way to end their unbearable misery other than death. Warren also discovered that many suicidal people just needed someone to talk to or a little help to get them through a temporary, but overwhelming, crisis. Believing that many suicides could be prevented, he openly sought suicidal people for counseling. Eventually the league had representatives in thirty-five cities across the nation, and it claimed to have saved at least one thousand lives each year.

Even though Warren's league was successful for more than forty years, his counselors remained among the few who tried to prevent suicide. Psychiatrists and psychologists shied away from suicidal patients for two reasons. First, most believed that they were ill-equipped to handle suicidal people, because there were no guidelines and few studies available to help them determine how best to treat such patients. Second, therapists feared failure, knowing that it could result in the loss of lives.

Prevention Through Analysis

In 1949, psychologists Edwin Shneidman and Norman L. Farberow began a scientific study of the prevention of suicide. They analyzed suicide notes, more than seven hundred in all, and talked at length to survivors and those who had attempted to take their own lives. After years of study and armed with many suggestions, they opened a suicide prevention center in Los Angeles, California, in 1958. They were joined by Robert E. Litman, a director of a psychiatric unit in a nearby hospital.

With no model to follow, the counselors at the Los Angeles Suicide Prevention Center had to make their own rules as they went along. They set up a hotline and asked for referrals from local psychiatrists and psychologists, who were greatly relieved to have someone to whom they could refer their suicidal patients. Then Shneidman and Farberow advertised their services to the community. They were quickly flooded with calls.

After working with a number of would-be suicide committers, prevention counselors developed a good sense of who was at great risk and needed to be hospitalized or watched around the clock until their crisis could be resolved. Eventually, the counselors developed tests that could identify these high-risk individuals.

Although the center's counselors did a lot of listening and gave out plenty of advice, they were not above doing the unthinkable in the counseling world if it would result in saving a life. For example, on one occasion, they threw a suicidal woman into a counselor's car, and they ordered her brother to sit on her until they reached the hospital.[1]

Robert Litman, Norman Farberow, and Edwin Shneidman formed the Suicide Prevention Center in 1958. In this photo, Litman (center) and Farberow (right) meet with the county coroner.

Expanding the Service Area

The Los Angeles Suicide Prevention Center was a successful model for preventive services. As more and more people sought its services, including people from other cities, additional communities decided to open similar facilities. Today, there are crisis centers and hotlines all over the country. They are listed on the web and in the Yellow Pages of telephone books, and most are operated twenty-four hours a day. Counselors, thanks to intensive training, are well equipped to handle questions and concerns regarding all types of crises, including suicide. Hotline callers can remain anonymous if they so choose, and they may call as often as they need.

Suicide prevention counselors take their crisis center jobs very seriously. As one said:

> There's no special magic that will give a caller a new life or that will keep a caller from committing suicide if he really wants to. All you can do is listen, really listen. That's what people need when they're hurting. You may think that listening's not very much, but you may be the first person to ever listen to them. And you may be the last.[2]

In addition to counselors in crisis centers, suicidal people today can receive help from school counselors, clergy, family physicians, and professional therapists who specialize in suicide prevention. Besides providing guidance, these professionals can put those thinking about suicide and actual attempters in touch with support groups. If drug or alcohol abuse is also a problem, counselors can make referrals to such groups as Alcoholics Anonymous and Narcotics Anonymous for additional help.

School counselors in particular play a key role in teen suicide prevention. As soon as a teen suicide takes place in a community, school counselors hold large group sessions on-site to discuss the event, help students deal with their grief, and try to assess the risk for more deaths in the school and the community itself. It may seem like a lot of effort to talk to thousands of students to ward

Thanks to the groundbreaking work of the successful Suicide Prevention Center, help is easy to find. Hotlines and Internet resources offer support regardless of location.

off potential suicides, but counselors consider saving even one life worth all of the hard work.

Learn From the Story of Charles

Unfortunately, even though many resources are available, not all people at high risk for suicide receive the counseling they need. Some, as already mentioned, believe that everything is hopeless, and they will refuse all offers of help. Others, like a teenager named Charles, are simply denied help.

Charles tried to hang himself. His parents did not take his attempt seriously, and when they brought him home from the hospital, they refused to contact the counselors and the suicide support group that the doctors at the hospital had recommended. Charles's mother insisted that the attempted hanging was just a silly misunderstanding.

For a while after his attempt, Charles, who was very good at masking his depression, seemed happier than before. He even joked about the rope marks on his neck. A few months later, however, he hanged himself again. This time, he successfully completed his suicide attempt.[3]

Charles's parents weren't the only ones to deny their child's problem. Study after study shows that parents believe that the thought of suicide has never crossed their children's minds. And even after an attempt is made, as many as 41 percent of parents who are told to get help fail to do so.[4]

Counseling is a must for suicidal patients. Whether it is given in or outside of a hospital setting, it is useful to help potential suicide attempters resolve their problems and find a reason to live. Often those who attempt suicide have previously put most of their energy into a job or a relationship. If they lose their position or their friend, they have nothing to fall back on until they can replace the loss. Counselors help suicidal people realize that they need to have more than one important thing in their lives, and they help them take steps to make that happen.

Patients are also encouraged to join a support group, for which fees, if they exist, are very low. At meetings, members—all of whom are or were suicidal—can share their feelings with others without the fear of being judged or ridiculed. Also, as members make progress, they serve as role models for incoming would-be suicide victims, giving members respect, status, and a reason to live.

Possible Roadblocks to Getting Help

Ideally, suicidal people should seek help on their own. Unfortunately, they seldom do. They may believe that having problems means that they've somehow done something wrong and, therefore, they deserve to be punished. Also, because they may have been deeply disappointed by others, suicidal people may be afraid to trust others or to reach out for help. They might believe that even if they ask, they are not likely to receive help. Or they might think that no one could possibly understand their pain or resolve their irresolvable problems.

Additional concerns come into play when suicide attempters are children. They might feel guilty about even thinking of going to someone other than their parents for help, because talking about their problems with strangers would betray their family and anger their parents. This is especially true if children have been ordered to keep certain events that occur in their home a secret.

If suicidal people won't seek advice, the most logical people to find help for them would be friends and relatives. Many do try to help their loved ones in need. Sometimes, though, suicidal people have become socially isolated. They have few friends, and their families may be one of the reasons that the would-be suicide attempters want to die. In such cases, these people are at the mercy of teachers, classmates, coworkers, or neighbors—anyone who might notice their distress and reach out to them.

Anyone who is considering suicide must seek the aid of a licensed counselor. This professional can provide a course of treatment, which might include alternative therapies such as support groups.

Many schools offer not only counseling, but suicide prevention workshops as well. In these workshops, students learn coping mechanisms for their emotions, as well as how to best help friends who are exhibiting signs of suicidal thoughts.

Know the Warning Signs

Since not all suicidal people behave in the same manner, the warning signs of an impending suicide vary from person to person. Even so, there are some common behaviors. In addition to being deeply depressed for some time and having a serious drug or alcohol problem, suicidal people may have experienced a traumatic event recently—serious trouble in school, for example—that has sent them reeling. They may also be obsessed with death and dying, and they may have talked about committing suicide. In addition, if

Triggering Events

Very stressful events can lead to depression or serve as a triggering event for suicide in an already deeply depressed person. Such events include:

- The death of a loved one or a hero especially if the death was due to suicide
- The loss of a valued position—a good job, for instance
- Serious trouble in school, failure or expulsion
- Difficulty with the law
- Public humiliation by peers or family members
- Failure to achieve a goal, particularly by individuals who tend to be perfectionists
- The onset of a painful, incurable illness
- An unplanned pregnancy
- The breakup of a romance
- Disruption in the home, a divorce, a remarriage, a move to another city, serious conflicts among family members

the person has made the decision to die, he or she, after months of feeling despondent and hopeless, may suddenly seem at peace.

Swing Into Action

If you think that someone you know is suicidal, it is important to take immediate action to try to save his or her life. Experts on suicide suggest that you begin by talking to the potential suicide attempter, listening to every word and watching facial expressions for clues. Repeat, in your own words, what you are told, making sure that you understand what is being said. For example, if the person says that he feels that his future is full of nothing but problems and then cites reasons for feeling this way, don't argue with him or deny his feelings. Saying "You think that your future holds nothing but problems" will at least make him aware that you heard what he said.

Ask him whether he is thinking about committing suicide. Don't hint or try to be subtle. Just say, "Are you thinking about killing yourself?" If he is thinking about dying, ask about a plan. The more detailed the plan, the more likely it is that this person is at high risk to try to end his life. If he has begun to act on his plan, giving away belongings, for example, or saying good-bye to classmates, his life is at great risk. Have someone stay with him until you can get help.

Even if a plan doesn't exist, seek help from an adult or a professional counselor at the earliest possible moment. Do not try to solve the problem yourself, believing that you have the skills to do so. Suicidal people are difficult to predict and more difficult to treat. Even professionals who deal with such patients every day are not always successful. This is not the time to take a chance.

Also, this is not the time to keep secrets. Betraying a confidence is difficult for anyone, especially teens, since they are intensely loyal to peers. Even if you have promised not to repeat what was said, remember that a life is at stake. Seek help from a trusted adult or call a crisis hotline.

While not a substitute for real treatment, having a serious discussion with a suicidal friend can show that he or she is not alone. If you suspect a friend or loved one is contemplating suicide, seek immediate help.

Project Semicolon

As punctuation, the semicolon represents a temporary pause before a sentence continues. A popular suicide prevention movement has adopted the semicolon as a symbol of hope, continuing on despite the temptation to end the sentence that is life.

Project Semicolon was begun in 2013 by suicide survivor Amy Bleuel, who lost her father to suicide. The project encourages people to draw a semicolon, or have one tattooed, on their skin as a sign of support to people struggling with mental illness, addiction, and, especially, thoughts of suicide. The organization's stated goal is to "achieve lower suicide rates in the US and around the world" by starting conversations about, and raising awareness of, the problem.

To share a story or learn more about Project Semicolon, go to http://www.projectsemicolon.org.

Treatment Options

Whether people are thinking about killing themselves or have already attempted to do so—there are thousands of failed suicide attempts each year—the recommended treatment depends on the risk. People at high risk for suicide may be hospitalized for a while. They are usually given medications such as tranquilizers to calm them or antidepressants to temporarily ease their emotional pain. Unless a brain-chemical imbalance is to blame for feeling suicidal, medications will not solve the suicidal person's problems, nor will they remove the risk of suicide. In most cases, medications simply make the high-risk individual more receptive to counseling.

Hospitalization provides several advantages. It gives suicidal people—and their loved ones—security, and it provides high-risk individuals with a quiet atmosphere in which to think about the crises that made them want to die. Also, unlike mental hospitals in the past, suicidal people now receive intensive counseling that can help them begin to resolve their problems.

On the other hand, hospitalization is not available to everyone. It can be very expensive, more than one thousand dollars a day in a private institution. Not all health insurance plans pay for confining suicidal patients, nor can all suicidal people or their families foot the bills. In addition, some states make it very difficult to hospitalize a patient against his or her will for more than several days, and some suicidal patients are not willing to be institutionalized.

Being There

Perhaps the best thing someone with a suicidal friend or family member can do is to make himself or herself available to listen. It is not easy, by any means, to hear that someone close to you wants to leave this earth permanently. But hopefully, by talking it out, the suicidal person might discover—on his or her own, or with your help—a reason to stick around and see what happens.

Sometimes dealing with people who apparently want to kill themselves requires asking some difficult questions. Asking point-blank if a friend is thinking about suicide can be as uncomfortable, if not more so, than listening. But friends do whatever it takes to help and support those for whom they care.

The following are some facts about suicide that readers might want to consider. First, people who talk about killing themselves must be taken seriously. Such behavior may be simply a cry for attention, but it is much more likely that these people plan to do away with themselves unless someone intervenes. Second, most depressed people have already thought about killing themselves. Chances are great that talking to them directly about suicide, depression, and dying will not be the one thing that pushes them over the edge. Doing so does, however, give you an opportunity to determine whether the person is likely to commit suicide and, if so, to get help. Third, it takes a long time to help suicidal people, the majority of whom are deeply depressed, find a reason to live. Sometimes progress is so slow. Encourage that person to keep going, even when it seems as if little or no progress is being made. Be prepared to support a suicidal friend for as long as it takes. Fourth, many suicidal people go on to lead happy, productive lives if they can find a reason to live. Above all else, there is hope.

Chapter Notes

Chapter 1: Suicide in the News

1. Lesley Messer, "Robin Williams Died in an Apparent Suicide by Hanging," ABC News, Aug. 2014, http://abcnews.go.com/Entertainment/robin-williams-apparently-committed-suicide-hanging/story?id=24947586 (accessed Sept. 2015).

2. Ben Chapman and Christina Boyle, "Staten Island Teen Amanada Cummings Kills Self by Jumping in Front of Bus After Being Bullied," *New York Daily News*, Jan. 2012, http://www.nydailynews.com/new-york/staten-island-teen-kills-jumping-front-bus-family-cites-bullies-article-1.1000243 (accessed Sept. 2015).

3. John Bacon, "Suspect of On-Air Murder of Journalists Kills Himself," *USA Today*, Aug. 2015, http://www.usatoday.com/story/news/nation/2015/08/26/reports-two-dead-virginia-shooting-live-tv/32391633/ (accessed Sept. 2015).

4. Robert Foyle Hunwick, "Desperate Chinese Turn to Mass Suicide in Protest," *USA Today*, May 2015, http://www.usatoday.com/story/news/world/2015/05/20/globalpost-chinese-suicides/27642891/ (accessed Sept. 2015).

5. Greg Zoroya, "The Suicide Crisis," *USA Today*, Oct. 2014, http://www.usatoday.com/story/news/nation/2014/10/09/suicide-mental-health-prevention-research/15276353/ (accessed Sept. 2015).

6. Laura Dolce, *Suicide* (New York: Chelsea House Publishers, 1992), p. 13.

Chapter 2: Suicide Through the Ages

1. George Howe Colt, *November of the Soul: The Enigma of Suicide* (New York: Scribner, 2006), p. 129–130.

2. Ibid., p. 130–31.

3. Johann W. Von Goethe, *The Sorrows of Young Werther*, ed. David E. Wellbery (New York: Suhrkamp Verlag, 1988), p. 37, 54, 62, 85–86.

Chapter 3: The Faces of Suicide

1. Centers for Disease Control and Prevention, National Center for Health Statistics, "Suicide," *Fastats*, May 28, 1998, http://www.cdc.gov/nchswww/fastats/suicide.htm (accessed Sept. 15, 1998); National Institute of Mental Health, "Suicide Fact Sheet," *Suicide Research Consortium*, July 1, 1998, http://www.nimh.nih.gov/research/suicide/htm (accessed Sept. 15, 1998).

2. Staff, "Global Health Observatory Data Repository: Suicide Rates, Data by Country," World Health Organization, http://apps.who.int/gho/data/node.main.MHSUICIDE?lang=en (accessed Sept. 2015).

3. Tara Parker Pope, "Suicide Rates Rise Sharply in U.S.," *The New York Times*, May 2013, http://www.nytimes.com/2013/05/03/health/suicide-rate-rises-sharply-in-us.html?_r=0 (accessed Sept. 2015).

4. Nancy J. Osgood, *Suicide in Later Life: Recognizing the Warning Signs* (New York: Lexington Books, 1992), p. 13.

5. Herbert Hendin, *Suicide in America* (New York: W. W. Norton & Company, 1982), p. 60.

6. George Howe Colt, *November of the Soul: The Enigma of Suicide* (New York: Scribner, 2006), p. 256.

7. Ibid., p. 248.

8. Evan Thomas, "The Next Level," *Time*, April 7, 1997, p. 28–35.

9. Gary Remafedi, "Homosexual Teens Are at High Risk for Suicide," in *Suicide: Opposing Viewpoints*, ed. Tamara Roleff (San Diego: Greenhaven Press, 1998), p. 63.

10. Gary Remafedi, ed., *Death by Denial: Studies of Suicide in Gay and Lesbian Teenagers* (Boston: Alyson Publications, 1994), p. 17.

11. Kathleen Gilbert, "Study: Gay Teens Five Times More Likely to Attempt Suicide," LifeSite News, Apr. 2011, https://www.lifesitenews.com/news/study-gay-teens-five-times-more-likely-to-attempt-suicide (accessed Sept. 2015).

12. Hugh Ryan, "There's a Suicide Problem Among Transgender Youths—and We Need to Help," TakePart.com, May 2015, http://www.takepart.com/article/2015/05/15/transgender-mental-health-services (accessed Sept. 2015).

Chapter 4: Reasons for Self-Harm

1. Nancy J. Osgood, *Suicide in Later Life: Recognizing the Warning Signs* (New York: Lexington Books, 1992), p. 17.

2. Leslie Laurence, "Time to Level With Teen-age Girls," *Oshkosh Northwestern*, January 10, 1995, p. D2.

3. Staff, "The Relationship Between Suicide and Bullying: What We Know and What It Means for Schools," April 2014, http://www.cdc.gov/violenceprevention/pdf/bullying-suicide-translation-final-a.pdf (accessed Sept. 2015).

3. George Howe Colt, *November of the Soul: The Enigma of Suicide* (New York: Scribner, 2006), p. 203.

4. Rick Nauert, "Depression's Chemical Balance Explained," Psyche Central, http://psychcentral.com/news/2006/11/09/depressions-chemical-imbalance-explained/398.html (accessed Sept. 2015).

5. Staff, "FastStats: Accidents and Unintentional Injuries," Centers for Disease Control and Prevention, http://www.cdc.gov/nchs/fastats/accidental-injury.htm> (accessed Sept. 2015).

6. Colt, p. 49.

7. Laura Dolce, *Suicide* (New York: Chelsea House Publishers, 1992), p. 30.

8. "Suicide Rate Leaps Among Black Teen-agers," *Oshkosh Northwestern*, March 20, 1998, p. A4.

9. Ritch C. Savin-Williams, "Verbal and Physical Abuse as Stressors in the Lives of Lesbian, Gay Male, and Bisexual Youths," *Suicide*, ed. Robert E. Long (New York: H. W. Wilson, 1995), p. 32.

10. Ibid., p. 33.

11. Ibid., p. 36–39.

12. Arden Dier, "Graphic Teen Suicide Reports May Spur Copycats," Newser.com, May 2014, http://www.newser.com/story/186258/graphic-teen-suicide-reports-may-spur-copycats.html (accessed Sept. 2015).

Chapter 5: Unthinkable Acts

1. Drew DeSilver, "Suicides Account for Most Gun Deaths," Pew Research Center, May 2013, http://www.pewresearch.org/fact-tank/2013/05/24/suicides-account-for-most-gun-deaths/ (accessed Sept. 2015).

2. Laura Unger and Chris Kenning, "Guns Most Deadly Choice in Suicide Attempts," *USA Today*, July 2013, http://www.usatoday.com/story/news/nation/2013/07/21/guns-most-deadly-choice-in-suicide-attempts/2572097/ (accessed Sept. 2015).

3. Renee Milligan, "The Death Toll," The Final Leap, http://www.thefinalleap.com/the-death-toll.html (accessed Sept. 2015).

4. Laura Dolce, *Suicide* (New York: Chelsea House Publishers, 1992), p. 16.

5. Bernard Frankel and Rachel Kranz, *Straight Talk About Teenage Suicide* (New York: Facts On File, 1994), p. 83–84.

6. Jerry Johnston, *Why Suicide?* (Nashville: Oliver-Nelson Books, 1987), p. 9.

7. George Howe Colt, *The Enigma of Suicide* (New York: Summit Books, 1991), p. 240.

Chapter 6: The Death With Dignity Debate

1. Michael Betzold, "The Selling of Doctor Death," *The New Republic*, May 26, 1997, p. 23.
2. Ibid., p. 26.
3. David Goodman, "Kevorkian Proposes Transplant," *Milwaukee Journal Sentinel*, June 8, 1998, p. 8A.
4. S. Van McCray, "Kevorkian Proposes to Furnish Organs from Assisted Suicide," Health Law and Policy Institute, written July 1998, https://www.law.uh.edu/healthlaw/perspectives/Bioethics/980715Kevorkian.html (accessed Sept. 2015).
5. David Van Biema, "Death's Door Left Ajar," *Time*, July 7, 1997, p. 30.
6. "Court Passes on Assisted Suicide Law," *Milwaukee Journal Sentinel*, October 15, 1997, p. 1A.
7. Kevin B. O'Reilly, "Physician-Assisted Suicide Legal in Montana, Court Rules," Jan. 2010, http://www.amednews.com/article/20100118/profession/301189939/6/ (accessed Sept. 2015).
8. Valerie Richardson, "New Mexico Court Strikes Down Ruling That Allowed Assisted Suicide," *The Washington Times*, Aug. 2015, http://www.washingtontimes.com/news/2015/aug/11/assisted-suicide-new-mexico-ruling-struck-higher-c/ (accessed Sept. 2015).

Chapter 7: Left Behind

1. Christopher Lukas and Henry M. Seiden, *Silent Grief: Living in the Wake of Suicide* (New York: Charles Scribner's Sons, 1987), p. 19.
2. Ibid., p. 32.
3. Ibid.
4. "Readers Reply: Suicide Devastating to Survivors," *Oshkosh Northwestern*, July 6, 1997, p. F5.
5. Ibid.

6. George Howe Colt, *The Enigma of Suicide* (New York: Summit Books, 1991), p. 431.

7. Lukas and Seiden, p. 111.

8. Jonathan Smith, "How Dare You Judge My Mom's Decision to Die," *Milwaukee Journal Sentinel*, June 22, 1997, pp. 1J, 2J.

Chapter 8: Prevention and Treatment

1. George Howe Colt, *November of the Soul: The Enigma of Suicide* (New York: Scribner, 2006), p. 295.

2. Ibid., p. 282–83.

3. Bernard Frankel and Rachel Franz, *Straight Talk About Teenage Suicide* (New York: Facts On File, 1994), p. 88–89.

4. Ibid., p. 92.

Glossary

alienated—The feeling of no longer being part of a group or society at large.

ancestral—Refers to something that has been handed down from relatives in the past.

asphyxiation—The process of stopping breath enough to pass out and die.

dignity—The quality of having self-control that makes one worthy of being respected.

hasten—To cause something to happen more quickly than normal.

inhibitions—Nervous feelings that cause someone to keep quiet and/or not act.

isolation—The state of being separated from others.

lingering—The act of staying around or living longer than expected.

mobility—The ability to move from one place to another.

rural—Of or relating to life in the country.

standard—An acceptable level against which items in the same category are measured.

trauma—Having emotional or mental problems because of a difficult or horrible experience.

treatment—The methods by which a person gets help for a mental, physical, or emotional problem.

upheaval—A major change that causes conflict, stress, or anger.

urban—Of or relating to life in the city.

For More Information

Alliance of Hope for Suicide Loss Survivors
823 Clinton Pl.
Evanston, IL 60201
(847) 868-3313
www.allianceofhope.org/

American Association of Suicidology
5221 Wisconsin Ave. N.W.
Washington, DC 20015
(202) 237-2280
www.suicidology.org/

American Foundation for Suicide Prevention (AFSP)
120 Wall St.
New York, NY 10005
(888) 333-2377 (toll free)
www.afsp.org

Canadian Association for Suicide Prevention (CASP)
285 Benjamin Rd.
Waterloo, ON N2J 374
(519) 884-1470, ext. 2277
suicideprevention.ca/

Centre for Suicide Prevention
105 12th Ave. S.E., Suite 320
Calgary, AB T2G 1A1
(403) 245-3900
www.suicideinfo.ca/

Suicide Prevention Resource Center
43 Foundry Ave.
Waltham, MA 02453
(877) 438-7772
www.sprc.org/

Websites

National Suicide Prevention Lifeline
www.suicidepreventionlifeline.org
The lifeline is accessible twenty-four hours a day, seven days a week to those who need emotional support.

Speaking of Suicide
www.speakingofsuicide.com/
This website features articles aimed at people contemplating suicide, their friends and family, those who survived suicide attempts, those who suffered loss through suicide, and mental health professionals.

Suicide Awareness Voices of Education (SAVE)
www.save.org
This site provides information on suicide prevention, depression, and coping with loss; resources such as brochures and a suggested reading list; and a National Outreach Network.

Know the Signs

www.suicideispreventable.org/

Based in California, this suicide prevention campaign aims to educate the public on how to recognize the warning signs of suicide, what to say to someone contemplating suicide, and where to turn to for professional help.

The Trevor Project

www.thetrevorproject.org/

This national organization provides a lifeline, guidance, and resources to young lesbian, gay, bisexual, transgender, and questioning (LGBTQ) individuals in crisis.

Further Reading

Asher, Jay. *Thirteen Reasons Why* (fiction). New York: Random House, 2012.

Esherick, Joan. *Suicide & Self-Destructive Behaviors*. Broomhall, PA: Mason Crest, 2014.

Gale editors. *The Right to Die* (At Issue: Civil Liberties). San Diego: Greenhaven Press, 2014.

Giddens, Sandra. *Frequently Asked Questions About Suicide*. New York: Rosen Publishing, 2009.

Grollman, Earl A. *Straight Talk About Death for Teenagers: How to Cope With Losing Someone You Love*. Boston: Beacon Press, 2014.

Haerens, Margaret. *Suicide* (Global Viewpoints). San Diego: Greenhaven Press, 2011.

Huddle, Lorena. *Teen Suicide*. New York: Rosen Publishing, 2011.

Marcovitz, Hal. *Teens & Suicide*. Broomhall, PA: Mason Crest, 2014.

Merino, Noel. *Assisted Suicide*. San Diego: Greenhaven Press, 2012.

Parks, Peggy J. *How Can Suicide Be Reduced?* San Diego: ReferencePoint Press, 2014.

Index